GREGORIAN Chant

SONGS OF THE SPIRIT

GREGORIAN CHANT: WHISPERS OF THE DOVE

Gregorian chant is named after Saint Gregory the Great, who is supposed to have received it directly from the Holy Spirit. Medieval book illuminations show Gregory with a dove sitting on his shoulder, singing into his ear. Musical notes are streaming from the mouth of the Dove into Saint Gregory's ear and out of his mouth.

GREGORIAN Chant

SONGS OF THE SPIRIT

EDITED BY HUSTON SMITH

FOREWORD BY THOMAS MOORE

PHOTOGRAPHS BY DAVID WAKELY

KQED
BOOKS

SAN FRANCISCO

Vice President for Publishing & New Ventures: Mark K. Powelson
Publisher: Pamela Byers
Managing Editor: Suzanna Brabant
Developmental Editor: David Hett
Research Assistants: Ellen Marcus, David Hett
Spanish Translations: Ellen Marcus
Book Design: Big Fish
Photographs: David Wakely
Cover Design: Big Fish

KQED President & CEO: Mary G. F. Bitterman

Educational and non-profit groups wishing to order this book at
attractive quantity discounts may contact KQED Books & Video,
2601 Mariposa St., San Francisco, CA 94110.

Library of Congress Cataloguing-in-Publication Data

Gregorian chant: Songs of the spirit / edited by Huston Smith; with contributions
by Don Randel...(et al.); photographs by David Wakely; foreword by Thomas Moore.
          p. cm.
"From the hit PBS special."
Includes bibliographical references, discography, and index.
ISBN 0-912333-13-8
          1. Chants (Plain, Gregorian, etc.)—History and criticism.
I. Smith, Huston. II. Randel, Don. III. Wakely, David.
ML3082.G74 1996
782.32'22—dc20

95-54018
CIP
MN

ISBN 0-912333-13-8

Manufactured in the United States of America
10 9 8 7 6 5 4 3 2 1

Cover photo: Masatomo Kuriya/Photonica

Distributed to the trade by Publishers Group West

Contents

❦

CONTENTS

Foreword

by Thomas Moore

GAIN AND AGAIN spiritual writers of the past describe the graceful human life as an intermingling of body, soul, and spirit. The soul finds its place in the middle, linking our physical existence with our mental life and keeping imagination alive in all that we do. The mediating soul also makes us human: It keeps our perspective at human scale, makes us sensitive to the voices of conscience, and helps us live intimate lives in relation to the natural world and in community.

The role of spirit in this trinity of experience is multifaceted. A spiritual life grants transcendent vision, a sense of values, deep questions of meaning and self-understanding, and a profound participation in the mysterious and inexplicable dimensions of life known only in mystical, ritual, or meditative conditions. The spirit allows us to expand beyond the limits of our personal situation where we can sustain a feeling of wonder about nature and a sense of community that extends all the way from family and friends to global interdependence.

Somewhere in the development of our Western culture—the whens, hows, and whys are complex and not my concern here—we lost that trinitarian view of ordinary life. Today we usually describe our experiences in dualistic terms: mind/body, spirit/matter, spirituality/materialism, consciousness/unconsciousness. In a dualistic world, we often find ourselves shifting maddeningly from one extreme to another, or identifying with one side of the split while denigrating the other side.

Very spiritual people may look down on the average "unconscious" person, while those devoted to the ideal of being normal and ordinary may poke fun at New Agers and "granola eaters." I received a letter once from

> "Chanting can be a remarkable stress reducing technique, as well as a very lovely meditation. If one does it well, one's body resonates in certain areas, attention becomes focused on sound, and one becomes very quiet, totally involved with one's whole being."
>
> **Erik Peper**
> ASSOCIATE DIRECTOR,
> INSTITUTE OF HOLISTIC
> HEALING STUDIES
> SAN FRANCISCO STATE
> UNIVERSITY

a man who lamented the fact that the majority of people weren't as evolved as he was and therefore there wasn't much hope for humanity.

I think that, generally, spirituality has been affected negatively by modern values. It's common to hear people describe their spiritual lives in the language of personal development, and the atmosphere of that ambitious approach is often thick with narcissism. For centuries, of course, spiritual guides have warned against ambition and self-aggrandizement in the spiritual process, but their warnings seem especially relevant, though unheeded, today.

Not only have we tended toward a developmental approach to spirituality as a result of our modern bias toward an evolutionary view of life, but we have also absorbed the personalistic philosophies of the age. Many times, when I'm scheduled to give a lecture in a church or bookstore, people will ask me if I'm going to talk about spirituality or religion. To me, the two are inseparable, but today many make an emotionally charged distinction between an objective institution and a subjective journey into the spirit.

When the middle realm of soul is still connected to the spiritual life, we don't set up oppositions between tradition and personal exploration; the two are inextricably involved with each other. Traditions offer guidance, so we don't have to be inventing the spiritual wheel again and again. Tradition takes us out of our narcissism and ambition, connecting us to teachers, writers, and practitioners of the past, establishing a vital community across the ages and across cultures.

Modern values have also convinced us to focus the spiritual life on issues of belief, understanding, moral principle, and method. Yet each of these, when pursued single-mindedly, tends to drive a wedge between the spirit and the soul. The spiritual life can harden into rigid dogma, narrow into excessively reductive interpretations, become cruel in its moralism, and lose humane values in its accent on method, school, teacher, and vocabulary. But when the lower, more mundane soul affects the way we engage our spirituality, belief turns into ever-deepening imagination, understanding into the fruitful contemplation of mystery, moralism into a refined and compassionate ethical sensitivity, and method into a thoroughly spiritual approach to ordinary living.

It is often said that the medieval cathedrals of Christendom were filled with beautifully painted and sculpted themes from the Bible to teach illiterate people the fundamentals of their religion. That explanation has never appealed to me. I suspect rather that the brilliant artisans that created the beautiful images knew the importance of *contemplating* sacred mysteries. Modernism has taken almost everything away from contemplation and given its full attention to function and explanation. A more soul-centered culture knows that the spiritual life is profoundly enhanced through the contemplation of sacred realities made available by the many arts and crafts associated with temples and festivals.

Jews, Christians, Hindus, Buddhists, and others have passionately told me stories of their treasured spiritual moments when the accent was on music, color, pageantry, tradition, stories, rituals, and food. The great secret about the spiritual life, lost to modernism's ambition and exaggerated attention to consciousness, is that the highest levels of spiritual realization are available in the most ordinary details of a plain, ordinary life of family, body, and sensation. Spirit is fulfilled only when it is intimately connected to body and soul.

It's in this context that I remember so fondly spending twelve years in a Christian monastic setting: getting up at 5 a.m., meditating for an hour, chanting the morning hours of the Divine Office and the Kyries and the Glorias of the Mass. Work, food, community, dress, study, and, above all, music, were integral to the spiritual life. I spent those many years living the liminality—on the threshold—of body and spirit, the most ordinary life and the most exalted spirituality, deep personal engagement and intense community.

Beginning in a monastery in Ireland when I was twenty, I taught, sang, conducted, and occasionally, very carefully on pipe organs and lesser instruments, accompanied Gregorian chant. Chant has a strong spiritual component, but it also addresses the soul—speaks directly to the heart, stays in the memory, and colors the activities of a life. It can't be reduced to meanings, interpretations, and moralisms, but it guides a person surely and beautifully to regions of spirit that are grounded and true.

Values of the soul, such as beauty, imagination, heart, connectedness, and ordinariness, enrich spiritual experience and give it a living, communal, and humane context. Without these steadying virtues of the soul, spirit can become brutal and neurotically disassociated from human life. When spirit and soul come together intimately, it's difficult to discern one from the other, but when they are separated, one may seem at odds with the other. Many times in history, religious zealots have burned beautiful books, destroyed precious paintings, and outlawed inspiring music in the name of spiritual purity.

In modern life it's easy to vacillate between the unconsciousness of materialism and enthusiasm for spiritual enlightenment. Gregorian chant, with its gentle modes and subtle rhythms, models a different way, a mediating path that has in it some soul and some spirit. It doesn't descend into muzak nor does it soar into extreme heights of transcendent aural preciousness. It is definitely spiritual music and yet it is full of soul.

I hope that the surprising end-of-the-century revival of interest in the chant comes from an intuition about the need for soul in our spiritual lives, and that such a promising intuition will spread to other aspects of our spiritual explorations. Currently, it seems that we can be enthusiastically moral and believing without being sensitive to the world around us. The chant could teach us to move more gracefully and more constantly between the higher reaches of spirit and the lower levels of ordinary existence. There is great beauty in that music, which can be lived as well as heard. ■

Introduction

by Huston Smith

N THE CINCINNATI airport for a plane change, I was walking from one gate to another when a sound, unfamiliar in airports, stopped me in my tracks. I was passing a lounge where the incessant football game was flickering over its bar, but instead of the raucous noise that usually issues from such alcoves, I was hearing Gregorian chant from the monastery in Spain whose monks had rocketed to fame—"gone platinum" as a *New Yorker* cartoon put it—through its liturgy. I was not the only one who was transfixed. A small band formed spontaneously to align themselves for three minutes with a different world.

It took me back to another airport scene the year before. Mickey Hart of the Grateful Dead, my wife, and I were at the Oakland Airport to say goodbye to the Gyuto (Tibetan) monks whom Mickey had brought to America for their third American tour. These tours had introduced a new phrase into the vocabulary of music—"multiphonic chanting" (from the capacity of these monks to sing solo, harmonic chords). We were keeping them with us as long as we could, but when the gate attendant signaled that our time was up, they grouped, and for three minutes, as the plane waited, they poured their deep organ-like chords over the airport's turbulence like oil over choppy water. As the last of them disappeared into the boarding chute, an old woman, visibly shaken, approached me and asked, "What was that?" When I explained that they were beaming a thank-you blessing to the country that had befriended them for three months, tears rolled down her cheeks.

The Greeks spoke of the music of the spheres, and the Gospel of John attests that the Word came first; but it was the Indians who extended these insights to the view that the world consists entirely of sound. It is *Nada*

Don't you think the human soul always longs for something that takes us out of ourselves, and out of this world? Don't you think that people get excited about participating in a tradition of a thousand years or longer? Of course, you'll say it's the New Age phenomenon, it's a crossover phenomenon...

Thomas Kelly

PROFESSOR OF MUSICOLOGY
HARVARD UNIVERSITY

Brahma, sound (*nada*), as sounded by its divine source (*Brahma*). Modern science agrees that the universe does indeed consist of vibrations, but sound is more than vibration. Distinct from white noise, sound is vibrations in harmonic proportions, and from the billions of vibrations that are possible, the universe shows an overwhelming preference for the few thousand that make harmonic sense. Why this preference? Plotinus, Pythagorean to the core, would have answered: because the One from which all things issue is beautiful, and music is a beautiful mode. "All music, based upon melody and rhythm, is the earthly representative of heavenly music," he wrote.

This takes us back to the music of the spheres, but humanly speaking, mysteries abound. Why is our sense of hearing so carefully differentiated (far more so than our visual sense)?

Why are the data we receive from our ears much more precise than those that we glean with our eyes?

Why is the frequency range of what we can hear tenfold wider than what we can see? Is there a message for us in that difference?

Why can musical harmony be quantified and converted into mathematical proportions, whereas the harmony in a landscape and painting cannot?

Why is our sense of balance located in our ears?

Why, at the time of death, is hearing the last of our senses to take leave of us?

An introduction is not the place to pursue such questions. What it can do is alert readers to what this book has in store for them.

Based on the hit PBS special, *Gregorian Chant: Songs of the Spirit*, produced by Barry Stoner and Bruce and Ellen Marcus, this book introduces the reader to the music of Gregorian chant through an in-depth meeting with Ismael Fernandez de la Cuesta, Spain's leading singer and choir director of Gregorian chant. A compact disc containing the complete music of the television program accompanies the book.

Beginning with a thoughtful Foreword by Thomas Moore, former monk and best-selling author, this book offers the reader an insightful look at Gregorian chant from different perspectives. Throughout the pages, evocative photographs depict the Spanish countryside and the monasteries in which the program was filmed and the music recorded. Pictures of ancient and modern chant manuscripts, chant choirs, and

medieval and modern monastic life provide a rich background for engaging essays, interviews, and commentaries.

Part One, Whispers of the Dove, encapsulates Gregorian chant's twenty century history. No one could more appropriately introduce that topic than Ismael Fernandez de la Cuesta, whose album, *Chant*, sold more than five million copies and ignited a worldwide explosion of interest in Gregorian chant. Former monk and choir director of the Abbey of Santo Domingo de Silos, Ismael Fernandez de la Cuesta is also a scholar of ancient music, a theologian, composer, President of the Spanish Musicology Society, and Professor of Musicology at the Royal Conservatory in Madrid. His essay presents Gregorian chant as a living rather than antiquated music. Sr. Fernandez describes to an interviewer his monastic life at the Abbey Santo Domingo de Silos in Spain. You will meet Don Randel, Professor of Musicology and Provost at Cornell University, who knew Ismael Fernandez de la Cuesta as a young man at the Santo Domingo Abbey. Together they studied ancient chant manuscripts and formed a lifelong friendship through the shared love of their subject. Margot Fassler, Director of Yale University's Institute of Sacred Music, and Peter Jeffery, Gregorian chant scholar and Professor of Musicology at Princeton University, provide a musicological guided tour of chant as it developed in both Western and Eastern Europe.

Part Two, Serenity in Song, explores the healing power of chant and the revival of spirituality in the modern age. Timothy Rayborn, of the University of Leeds, England, presents an overview of the use of chant in five major world religions: Hinduism, Buddhism, Judaism, Christianity, and Islam. Dr. Kenneth R. Pelletier, of the Stanford University School of Medicine, offers an insightful view of the physical, psychological, and even spiritual benefits of listening to Gregorian chant.

Part Three, Rediscovering Gregorian Chant in the New Millennium, explores the enduring appeal of Gregorian chant. Noted musicologist Richard Crocker presents an essay on the attraction of Gregorian chant to modern listeners. A listening guide for *Alma redemptoris mater*, a selection from the CD included with this book, is provided by Robert Winter, Chairman of the Music Department at UCLA. The guide will help the reader understand and follow the musical patterns of the piece. A final essay, by Ismael Fernandez de la Cuesta, provides background information on the CD's entire program.

Throughout the book are commentaries and interviews with people from all walks of life that attest to the power that Gregorian chant continues to exert on the Western public.

The prophet Isaiah once promised his people, "Hear, and your soul will live." His promise holds for this book, and its accompanying music, as well. ■

1

Whispers of the Dove

A Living Tradition

TWENTY CENTURIES OF GREGORIAN CHANT

by Ismael Fernandez de la Cuesta

REGORIAN CHANT IS one of several diverse forms of Christian liturgical chant practiced in the Mediterranean West. In the first century AD, Christians met weekly to commemorate the Lord's Supper with the Apostles, as Jesus had instructed them to do. Songs and prayers used by the early Christians were the same ones used by the Jews in their liturgy. Passages from the Bible were read in synagogue, and psalms and canticles from the Old Testament were recited. Historical accounts from the Bible and lyric poems written in verse were intoned in a special way, so that worshippers could hear and memorize the texts more readily. Traditional Jewish communities continued their recitations in Hebrew, but Jews who lived in densely populated areas began to recite in Greek. Christians also normally used Greek when reciting from the Bible. However, in the Mediterranean West, Christians began to recite in the vernacular Latin so that the verses would be easily understood by everyone. In areas where Christians flourished, many different versions of the most common biblical texts were created as passages were translated from Greek into Latin. From these diverse translations, numerous Latin texts arose—each with unique wording. The diversity of the texts resulted in many regional variations within the intoned poetry and prose.

Recitation evolved as readers or cantors imposed their own styles. A repertory of chants was formed fairly rapidly and seems to have been almost complete by the sixth century. We have evidence of diverse repertories: Roman and "Old Roman" chant in Rome and within its zone of influence;

Beneventan chant in the south of Italy; Ambrosian chant in Milan; Hispanic (later called "Mozarabic") chant in Spain; and Gallican chant in France.

In the eighth century, the emperors, desiring to increase their political influence, initiated unification of liturgy and chant throughout the Western world. Chants from the basilica of the Pope in Rome were chosen as the official repertory. To force supremacy of this chant over all the other chants practiced in Europe at the time, the composition of the Roman chants were attributed to Saint Gregory the Great, who was said to have written each and every piece by divine inspiration. From then on, Christian liturgical chant became known as Gregorian chant. Except for resistance from some of the regional churches, for example in Milan and Spain, Gregorian chant was accepted by all Western European Christians.

Gregorian chant has been practiced without interruption by Catholic Christians to modern day. Passage of time and diversity of communities where chants have been sung account for the almost infinite number of variants within the repertory. Since the ninth century, Gregorian chant has represented the repertory on which modern music theory is based. From the Gregorian body of works came the major innovations of technique that ultimately led to the composition of Western culture's greatest masterpieces. Musical notation, modes, scale, polyphony, counterpoint, and consonant harmony have their beginnings in the Gregorian chant. Thus, for composers of the twelfth through seventeenth centuries and beyond,

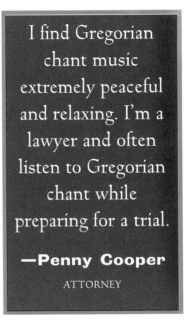

I find Gregorian chant music extremely peaceful and relaxing. I'm a lawyer and often listen to Gregorian chant while preparing for a trial.

—Penny Cooper
ATTORNEY

Gregorian chant was the model, the source of inspiration—even the very material of their works. One difference between the music of the Occidental culture and that of other very refined cultures, such as Chinese or Arabic, is that in the Orient there was no basic repertory such as the Gregorian chant upon which to create musical works or to establish compositional techniques that could be perfected over time.

So we see that Gregorian chant is the basic foundation of musical culture in the West. This music represents a deep-seated reality within our collective "subconscious." It is no wonder, then, that Gregorian chant recently has reemerged—this time in an explosive manner—throughout the entire world. ∎

The Evolution of a Chant Manuscript

*A fragment of the Introit (entrance Chant) Spiritus Domini, presented in square notation.
An example of modern musical notation appears on the opposite page.*

Spiritus Domini replevit
orbem terrarum, alleluia:
et hoc quod continet omnia,
scientiam habet vocis,
alleluia, alleluia. alleluia.

The Spirit of the Lord fills
the whole orb of earth, alleluia:
and that which contains all things
has knowledge of the voice,
alleluia, alleluia, alleluia.

Mozarabic Chant

by Bruno Stablein

IT WAS NOT until after the end of the first millennium that the Gregorian liturgy of the Roman papacy finally achieved universal acceptance. Until that time, Western Europe had accommodated a wide variety of liturgies, each of which was influenced, at least in part, by the ethnic characteristics and prevailing social structure of regional populations: the ancient Gallician rite of the Merovingian state religion, the Celtic liturgy of countless Irish monasteries, the liturgy adopted in Milan, which for centuries was Italy's most powerful city, the courtly ceremonial of the Langobardic Dukes in southern Italy, the two rites of the Roman liturgy, and, finally, the liturgy of the Iberian peninsula, which deserves special attention because of its colorful nature and highly developed individuality, due in no small part to Spain's national character.

The old Toledan rite flourished during the seventh century in what was then the kingdom of the Visigoths, with its political center and, hence, its ecclesiastical center, in Toledo. It owed its development less to the well known polymath Isidore of Seville (d. 636) than to Toledo's three leading prelates and poet-musicians, the Visigothic nobleman Eugenius III and his successors, Ildefonse and Julian. Although the Visigoth kingdom was overrun by the Arabs in 711, seven centuries of Moorish rule brought few changes in religion and ritual. In general, Christians were not prevented from practicing their faith. They were even described as Arabs or, rather, as *moz* Arabs (literally, "false" Arabs), hence the designation of their Visigothic rite as Mozarabic.

The situation did not change until after 1000, when the gradual reconquest of the peninsula led to the suppression and eventual extirpation of the old indigenous Visigothic and Mozarabic liturgy and its chants, all of which had been allowed to flourish under the Moors. It is necessary, therefore, to distinguish between two different liturgies, namely the Mozarabic liturgy (also described as "Hispanic" or "Visigothic") and the Roman liturgy, which slowly came to dominate the whole of the Iberian peninsula in the years after 1050.

Vestiges of the Mozarabic rite survived through oral tradition (a tradition incomparably more reliable in the Middle Ages than any other form of transmission). It was thanks to one of Spain's greatest national figures, Cardinal Jimenez de Cisneros (d.1517), that this tradition was salvaged, in two different ways: the melodic formulas sung by the priest during Mass, or in alternation with him, were printed by Jimenez in 1500 (more recently and more accessibly, reprinted in volume 85 of Migne's *Patrologia Latina*), while the actual melodies were transcribed in three great choirbooks currently lodged in the Mozarabic Chapel in Toledo Cathedral. Twenty-three of them were reproduced by Casiano Rojo and German Prado, two Benedictine monks from Silos, in a monograph first published in 1929. It remains a standard work on the subject.

Whereas the majority of the melodies published in the 1500 collection may be regarded, at least on stylistic grounds, as genuinely Hispanic, the same cannot be said of the chants contained in the choirbooks. It has been noted, for example, that their melodies differ from the older neumatizations, even though the texts themselves are virtually identical. Nonetheless, it has to be said that they breathe a palpably "Mozarabic" spirit, that they cannot be placed in any of the stylistic categories known to have existed around 1500, and that we appear to be dealing, therefore, with what might be termed neo-Mozarabic melodies. If they are not all genuine, at least some of them may be so. (Scholars have yet to pronounce the final word on the matter.) ■

Ismael Fernandez De La Cuesta

Translated from Spanish by Ellen Marcus

OU BEGAN YOUR studies at the Benedictine Monastery of Silos when you were ten. Did you study Gregorian chant at that early age?

Fernandez de la Cuesta Yes. When I was a little boy my parents brought me to the monastery to attend elementary school and to earn my *bachillerato* degree. I studied Gregorian chant and music from the beginning. Like all the boys at Silos, I learned very young how to interpret *neumes* (Gregorian chant's notational signs). And, when I arrived, they made me a boy chorister. So I've been a singer of Gregorian chant since the age of ten.

What was it like to be in the monastery of Silos at that time?
Fernandez de la Cuesta I liked it there. To me, it was truly amazing. In post-war Spain there were very few chances to study, and as soon as I arrived, I had the opportunity to examine the human sciences and pursue humanistic studies. I felt extremely fortunate to be in such an extraordinary and ancient learning center.

Were there more monks at Silos when you were a boy than there are now?
Fernandez de la Cuesta Oh, many more. Forty or fifty monks—mostly older men. The intellectual and spiritual life there was really very, very great.

When I was in high school, my French teacher lent me a collection of chant records, most of them from the Abbey of Solesmes, in France. The chants were so peaceful and calming, I would listen to them when I needed to quiet down and make a calm place in my life. I still listen to Gregorian chant because it is a still point in a turning world.

Rose M. Atiyeh

U.S. GOVERNMENT EMPLOYEE,
CHURCH MUSICIAN

How did you become the choir director at Silos?

Fernandez de la Cuesta I had come back to Silos after studying theology, Gregorian chant, and music at the monastery of Solesmes, in France, and I was—according to the abbot—ready to conduct the choir. Solesmes is the place where I learned almost everything I know about Gregorian chant. Their style is the authentic Gregorian chant style of centuries ago. Silos is really a derivative, an offspring, of the great monastery of Solesmes, which is truly the greatest center of Gregorian chant study in our time.

In the late nineteenth century, all over Europe there was a return to performing a style of Gregorian chant that could be considered the "classical" style. This occurred, in large part, because of the extraordinary scholarly work done by the monks of Solesmes. They initiated the strenuous musicological task of studying the chant in depth. They continue today a meticulous study of this music, their goal being to find the Gregorian chant style as it was performed in ancient times, back when the earliest manuscripts were written. I think this work is extremely interesting and important, but also I should mention—as Father Pothier, the creator of the Solesmes school used to say—that not only were those early centuries important for Gregorian chant, but *all* centuries were important. And that includes the twentieth century, which has produced its own way of interpreting Gregorian chant, thanks mainly to the Solesmes monks.

Those of us who were at Silos generally followed the Solesmes tradition. Back then, before the changes made by the Church after the Second Vatican Council, everyone sang Gregorian chant, and *only* Gregorian chant—at least in the monasteries and great cathedrals. When I came back to Silos from Solesmes, I began to conduct and sing with the choir, establishing a new way of chanting. What I did was change the rhythm of the chants so there would be no trouble with the unification of the voices in a choir. At the same time I had to keep in mind the development of the melody and the meaning of the texts; to form phrases that communicated the essence of the text; to preserve the phrases that were meant for prayer. But, as a foundation for the text, I had to maintain a very precise rhythm. This is the style you have heard on our recordings, and it is the same style my choir uses now.

On your latest recording, you have included a Mass of the Virgin Mary. Why did you choose this particular mass?

Fernandez de la Cuesta   I chose it precisely because it *is* a *Missa de Beata Virgine*—a Mass of the Virgin Mary. Every Saturday, the *Missa Beata Virgine* used to be sung. It was a very important mass composed of pieces taken from various manuscripts. I also chose several Marian antiphons for this performance.

When devotion to the Virgin Mary was established, it was a moment in history when the music of the troubadour and of love—meaning the love of a woman—were very significant. At this same time, Christians and clergy worshipped Mary, expressing their love for a woman in Heaven. The chants I am presenting now (the *antifonas marianas*) appeared in the twelfth, thirteenth, and fourteenth centuries and are very extraordinary, very old, and of great beauty.

Why do you believe Gregorian chant became so very popular after the release of the Chant CD?

Fernandez de la Cuesta   I think there are several reasons for its popularity, and each of them go well beyond the commercial process of marketing the music. To begin with, Gregorian chant is a music that carries an important spiritual message to people who are not finding other meaningful messages from music. The message of Gregorian chant is about man's life in relation to God, to all that we cannot see. That is something quite different from what we know from this life on earth.

What is the origin of Gregorian chant?

Fernandez de la Cuesta   The origin is very difficult to establish because it grew in a spontaneous and natural way from the ancient Jewish tradition of chanting the Psalms, which Christians continued. The master singers began to embellish the musical recitations, and from this practice grew the more intricate forms that we hear today in Gregorian chant.

During the Carolinian Empire, there was a desire by the political powers in Rome to centralize, to unify, the chant tradition. This was based on the evangelical principle of St. Peter, the first bishop of Rome and the first of the Apostles. But this effort at unifying did not prevent each tradition, or even each regional church, from developing their own chant repertory. For example, in Spain there was an unique Hispanic chant, later called "Mozarabic" chant, which lasted until the eleventh century.

All the regional traditions fundamentally grew out of the same simple reality: There were different translations of the Book of Psalms from Hebrew into Greek into Latin, these different versions of the text producing different music. Because if *laudatio* is the translation chosen instead of *jubilatio*, in one instance I will be pronouncing a four-

syllable word and in the other a five syllable word. And since each chant established itself with different vocabulary, the music had to change slightly. This is how different traditions were established.

When an attempt to unify the chant occurred in the Carolinian era, everyone basically accepted a sort of *textus receptus* which came from the Imperial Court of the Emperor. In reality, once the Gregorian chant was unified throughout Christendom, each region went on to again produce distinct variations, due to the differences in styles of singing. So by the sixteenth century, around the time of the Council of Trent, the Pope once more had to order the various traditions to conform with Gregorian chant. But this standardization is something that has never been possible to achieve fully.

Historically, Gregorian chant is extraordinarily important because it is the foundation, the creative base, for all Western music. Classical music has its roots in Gregorian chant. Polyphony began with discant, the simple ornamentation of Gregorian chant. Discant eventually existed independently from Gregorian chant, and this phenomenon constituted a special polyphonic technique from which harmony was derived in the West. Thanks to this technical advance, our culture produced great composers of polyphonic music: Palestrina, Lassus, Victoria, Josquin des Pres, and of course Bach and Mozart.

Many people think of Gregorian chant as only unison singing, not discant.
Fernandez de la Cuesta *Discanto* is a part of the whole of Gregorian chant repertory. It was sung in many monasteries, even though there are no early manuscripts to show it because ornamentation upon the chant was not written into the music. What is preserved in the manuscripts is the *essence* of each chant. Precisely how the master singers sang each piece, we have no way of knowing. We don't have any tapes or records of them, do we? On some ancient codices there are cryptic little signs, the meaning of which can be deciphered only with great difficulty, and even then, not with great precision. So the manuscripts convey to us only a small part of what the music really was.

However, the discant is first and foremost an *ornamentation* upon the Gregorian chant. In my interpretations of Gregorian chant currently being presented, I have included the discant because I believe these discants *are* Gregorian chant in the purest sense of those two words. Gregorian chant is not a dead music; it is always new and always modern. And throughout the course of its long history, it gained ornamentation that corresponded to the musical tastes of each century—this is true up to and including today. Gregorian chant is not an antiquated chant. It is an old chant, but not one that has ever died or disappeared. Since the time of the ancient Jews, and then throughout the era of Christianization, and up to today, Psalms have been sung, and Gregorian chant has been chanted. It has been alive. While other types of music have endured for a while, they have eventually disappeared. Those of us who are musicologists dig up ancient music because that's what we like to do, just as an archeologist will enjoy unearthing an ancient monument. But this is not the way it is with Gregorian chant, because this music has been constantly alive and changing—in the second century, in the third century, in the sixth century, in the twelfth century, in the sixteenth century, and in the twentieth century. It has always been a contemporary phenomenon.

It's clear that you love Gregorian chant very much.

Fernandez de la Cuesta I love all good music. Absolutely all of it. I like modern and ancient music, and I'm especially fond of the great polyphonists. I like Guillaume de Machaut, I like Palestrina, I like Victoria—I really love Bach, Monteverdi, and also Mozart, Beethoven, and of course Manuel de Falla.

But there is something about Gregorian chant that has a special place in your heart.

Fernandez de la Cuesta Yes. It communicates. Gregorian chant is a chant designed in the first place for prayer, for expressing human emotion, perhaps to a greater degree than any other kind of music. Remember, it has a very important feature to it—it has a text. This text has been sung, has been written, and has been used now for forty centuries, going back into ancient Jewish times and enduring to the present. This long history enhances its humanistic content. But, most importantly, Gregorian chant expresses musically all that is *contained* in the text. Gregorian chant has extraordinary spiritual power. That is why I love it. ■

anquam sponsus dominus pro
propterea benedixit te deus in eter
num. ps. Eructavit.

Monastic and Popular Chant

by Don Randel

REGORIAN CHANT IS, to me, extraordinarily beautiful music. Part of its beauty has to do with its tradition and its association with beautiful texts—in the main from the Psalms, but not exclusively—and the way it has been integrated with a way of life. It is music that has a very powerful aesthetic appeal and, at the same time, an ordering power with respect to life itself.

I came to the study of Gregorian chant as a student of the history of music, rather than as a practitioner or adherent to the religion which gave birth to it. My first encounter with Gregorian chant in the lives of the people who make it was as a student in Spain, where I went to study manuscripts from the Middle Ages. I drove up to this little monastery out in the middle of Castile, which was quite off the beaten path and not known to tourists. And there I was met at the door by a young monk, Ismael Fernandez de la Cuesta, who, having grown up in that part of the world, and having spent most of his life in that monastery, was interested in the same manuscripts as was I from thousands of miles away. There began a friendship and a scholarly collaboration that has meant a great deal to me over the years.

The monks at the Monastery of Santo Domingo de Silos made me welcome. Then, as now, Gregorian chant was an organizing force in their lives. They invited me to be a part of their community. I ate with them, attended services, studied the ancient manuscripts, and talked far into the night with the monk who became my friend and who was as interested and as eager as I to talk about the repertory that he sang every day.

Ismael was at that time the choirmaster at the monastery. Although only in his mid-twenties, he had already assumed a position of leadership with the choir, singing alongside people who were in their seventies and who had been singing that repertory for fifty or sixty years. He was conducting and training the choir, and bringing its younger members into the performance of the chant on a daily basis. He had studied at Solesmes, the great French monastery which is the principle house in the Benedictine world, charged with the preservation and study of Gregorian chant. The Benedictines have a wonderful tradition of scholarship, which Ismael reflected. He was both a scholar and a performer from his earliest days. Over time, he has kept up both of these activities, and he is now the Professor of Gregorian chant at the conservatory in Madrid and at the same time is leading a choir that performs both Gregorian chant and some slightly later repertories built upon the chant.

Chant, the compact disc that has become so popular in the last few years, was actually recorded in the early seventies in this little monastery in north-central Spain. In my view, it is a wonderful example of the real thing—not the only possible example, but an example of music recorded by people whose life was built around the singing of it. In that sense, *Chant* has a quality of authenticity about it that not every recording of Gregorian chant does. You can find recordings of Gregorian chant made in other countries that sound quite different. Part of that is because people in France and Spain and Germany and Italy have different ways of pronouncing Latin. That alone has a big effect on their singing. But there is also a style and tradition of singing associated with Spain that makes itself felt in these recordings.

The popularity of this and other recordings of Gregorian chant is remarkable to musicologists like myself. What is striking is the quite astonishing leap of Gregorian chant out of its liturgical context into a wholly secular context. People who bought *Chant*, who have or will watch the PBS program *Gregorian Chant: Songs of the Spirit*, or buy this book, with its new CD, have not come to Gregorian chant primarily because it is something that serves the worship of the church. Gregorian chant, instead, has shown a direct *musical* appeal, quite independent of its explicit liturgical context.

How one is to explain that appeal is not easy. One might hope it has to do with a return to spiritual values, although that might be too facile of an explanation. It certainly is an appealing alternative, or complement, to lots of other kinds of music that we hear in the world. ■

Floor Plan of a Medieval Monastery

by Robert Winter

The monastery built during the ninth century in the tiny village of St. Gall in Switzerland was one of the most famous in western Europe. St. Gall himself was thought to be one of several Irish monks who visited the area in the early seventh century. The local duke, after tolerating three years of vigorous proselytizing by the monks, at last ordered them to leave. Illness prevented St. Gall from leaving with his companions, however, and he retired to a steep cliff overlooking a river. There he resolved to spend his last days in fasting and prayer. He lived long enough to win fame as a preacher and managed to convert many of the local residents to Christianity. When he died, he was buried with some of his relics in a tiny hermitage he had built for himself.

After his death, St. Gall's reputation spread far and wide, and pilgrims came to visit the hermitage. By the middle of the eighth century, two priests, a deacon, and 47 monks had taken up residence at the hermitage, now vastly expanded. In time, a Benedictine abbey was erected near the original site. Under Abbot Gozbert (d.836), St. Gall was transformed into one of the most impressive monasteries in Europe. Although little of the structure survives, the original plans have been preserved. They reveal a design that was typical of large, prosperous abbeys of the time. The sanctuary had stained-glass windows and chandeliers, and the altars were decorated with gold and silver and covered with expensive cloth. Frescoes (plaster painted while still fresh, creating deep, rich images) adorned the walls. St. Gall lay only a few miles from the intersection of two major trade routes, and visitors filled the sanctuary to attend the two Masses celebrated each day.

Nearby was a well-stocked library, several large kitchens (for guests of varying social status), an inn for pilgrims and one for noble guests (another arrangement hard to reconcile with Christian beliefs), a bakery and brewery, artisan workshops, a flour mill, a wood turning shop, a wheelwright's shop, a barn (with room for sheep, goats, cows, horses, and pigs), a school, a hospital, and numerous outbuildings.

During its prime in the tenth century, the abbey received countless bequests of land and even whole monasteries. Some of these bequests were no doubt made by pious Christians, though others were probably made in the hope of selling supplies to the hundreds of people who now lived at the abbey. (Some donors specified that their bequests were to go into effect only after their deaths.) It is difficult to reconcile all this with the Benedictine vow of poverty, but the abbots doubtless felt that the abbey's wealth testified to the glory of God.

In the famous school of St. Gall, founded in the eighth century, apprentices learned to read and write and to copy and illuminate manuscripts in the *scriptorium* (the writing room). The monks studied the movement of the sun and stars and kept abreast of the most recent developments in science. They could study painting, architecture, sculpture, weaving, and spinning.

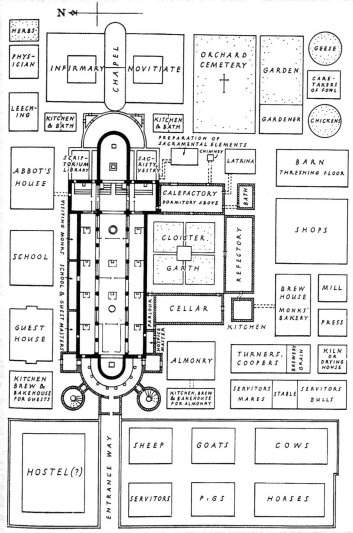

Plans for the Monastery of St. Gall: The plans reveal a design for a self-sufficient community, complete with a cemetery that doubled as an orchard. The calefactory was a heated sitting room; in the almonry, alms were distributed to the poor.

The curriculum also included instruction in the theory and composition of music, as evidenced by the rich collection of music manuscripts that has survived. One monk, Notker Balbulus (Notker the Stammerer; ca. 840–912), was a well-known musician at St. Gall who, according to one account, introduced a form of chant known as *sequence*, long syllabic settings of unrhymed verses based on lengthy melismas from the chant. Notker's aim, according to the account, was to help the monks memorize long musical passages.

Over time, the abbots turned over much of the farming to apprentices or neighboring peasants in order to free time for scholarly pursuits. They stocked their library with books in Latin and Greek and collected German literature. (Most of the abbots were members of the German nobility.)

St. Gall was not immune from the violence of the outside world, however. One ninth-century abbot, who kept a chronicle that has come down to us, reminds us of the fragility of medieval life—and also reminds us that the Christian dictum to "turn the other cheek" had its limits:

> The Saracens, whose nature it is to be strong in the mountains, molested us and our dependents from the south to such an extent that, having gained possession of our grazing lands and mountains, they even hurled javelins at the monks following the cross (i.e., in a procession) around the town. The Abbot's troops could not discover where they were hiding. One night he himself, accompanied by the boldest men from among the attendants, found where their hiding place was, and attacked them in their sleep with spears, sickles, and axes. Some were killed, others taken prisoner, and the rest escaped by flight; (the abbot) considered it useless to pursue them, since they ran over the mountain more swiftly than goats. But he drove the captives before him to the monastery. Since, however, they refused to eat or drink, they all perished. It will suffice to mention this as an example of the sufferings of that time... for if I were to list all the hardships which our community suffered at the hands of the Saracens, I should fill a volume. ■

The Development of Gregorian Chant in Europe

by Margot Fassler and Peter Jeffery

HE EARLIEST CHRISTIAN music developed from a variety of traditions, but most especially from the Jewish custom of singing at gatherings around a meal. In fact, the most distinctive services of the early church were not Christianized synagogue or Temple gatherings, but rather the common meals attended by groups of disciples and the family-centered meals similar to those surviving in today's Jewish homes, especially the Friday-night supper that opens the Sabbath and the Passover seder.

One reason that the Temple is not likely to have been the immediate source of early Christian music is that the elaborate Temple worship, with its animal sacrifices, professional priests, and levitical "orchestra," could not have been duplicated in the restricted conditions of early Christian homes and gathering sites.

Among the pagans, too, banquet meals were the occasion for religious and philosophical discussion, as well as for religious and secular song.

The banquet gatherings celebrated by the early church were seen as commemorating, and in a sense continuing, the meals Jesus himself had celebrated with his disciples, and it was from such gatherings that the Christian Eucharist service developed.

The oldest sources describe early Christian music as "psalms, hymns, and spiritual songs" (Ephesians 5:18). These words probably did not actually refer to distinct musical genres. Nonetheless, their use helps to distinguish the three essential types of texts that were sung during the early

period. These are psalms, namely the 150 Psalms of the Bible; canticles, psalm like poems found in *Exodus*, *Habakkuk*, and other Bible books; and hymns, or nonscriptural compositions of any kind. The earliest Christian hymns, while resembling the psalms and canticles in form and structure, deal with the identity of Christ or the meaning of his life and death.

THE CONVERSION OF THE ROMAN EMPIRE

Upon Emperor Constantine's conversion at the beginning of the fourth century, Christians became free to leave their house-churches and worship openly. As a result, the liturgy began to develop in two new directions, cathedral liturgy and monastic liturgy.

With the end of persecution, great basilicas, modeled on imperial courthouses and designed to hold the large crowds of new Christian worshipers, were built throughout the empire. On major feasts, it was the practice for a city's entire Christian community, under the leadership of the bishop, to gather together in a church and from there to march in procession to the basilica, where the Eucharist would be celebrated. The most important services, reserved for the most solemn days, were at the cathedral, the bishop's "headquarters," where his *cathedra* (chair) was located.

With its large crowds, numerous clergy, lengthy processions, and impressive surroundings, cathedral liturgy soon became much more elaborate and formalized than in the days of the house-churches. The bishop was an imperial as well as a church official, and the liturgy began to absorb some of the secular ceremony that the bishop's new status entitled him to use. For example, when he entered the basilica at the beginning of a service, he had the right to be met by a choir, a practice that may have developed into what we today know as the *introit*.

Congregational singing was important at this early date. Most often, a soloist sang the verses of a psalm, and the congregation joined in at the end of the verse with an unvarying refrain. This type of psalmody is first mentioned in connection with vigils, services that lasted much of the night and ended in the morning.

Two other types of psalmody figured prominently in the early cathedral liturgy, *antiphonal* and *direct*. In antiphonal psalmody two choirs, or two halves of the congregation, took alternate turns singing verses, including a refrain at the end of the verse. In direct psalmody the entire refrain was sung straight through by all.

Many lay Christians of the time, of both sexes, longed for a more rigorous and heroic spirituality than the emerging civic Christianity. They found it in the wilderness outside the cities.

In the deserts of Egypt, laymen or laywomen grouped together in Christianity's first monastic communities, unceasing prayer their ideal. Most psalms were chanted by a soloist while other monks listened, although the final psalm was responded to by the entire community with the word *Alleluia*.

Originally, the monastic communities, which housed few or no clergy, were reluctant to use the nonscriptural hymns of the cathedrals, with their beautiful poetry and melodies. This reluctance gradually weakened as the cathedral and monastic types of worship began to merge.

THE EARLY MEDIEVAL SYNTHESIS

Even while they were first emerging, the cathedral and monastic types of worship were influencing each other. Some monastic communities, established in or near cities, participated in cathedral services in addition to their own. Monks, who originally had been laymen, became increasingly clericalized. The synthesizing of cathedral and monastic elements was creating a hybrid we would come to know as the fully formed liturgy of the Middle Ages.

As liturgical traditions began to be written down and organized into books, literacy and education became a largely clerical preserve. Liturgical concerns were looked upon as activity carried out by clerics on behalf of the whole church, rather than as an act of the assembly. More of the responsibility for singing fell to the choir, made up of low ranking clergy. While congregational singing and other forms of participation did not completely die out during the Middle Ages, it was inevitable that the role of the laity in public worship would diminish. Not surprisingly, most of the liturgical music that we have from the Middle Ages is the music of cathedrals, monasteries, and the other clerical and religious communities that were so numerous during the medieval period.

> Some of the most hauntingly beautiful music ever penned, Gregorian chant has influenced every part of Western civilization. It is the inspirational seed for all musical forms, religious and secular, that have followed, including operas, symphonies, musicals, even popular music and jazz.
>
> **Lotfi Mansouri**
> GENERAL DIRECTOR
> SAN FRANCISCO OPERA

THE MEDIEVAL REPERTORIES

Every city or region seems to have developed its own chant repertory, with text, prayers, readings, and other materials ordered in standardized cycles according to the local liturgical calendar.

The first real chant book, containing the texts of all the scriptural and nonscriptural chants and arranged by the date and time each was to be sung during the year, was compiled at Jerusalem, probably during the seventh century. It survives only in a Georgian translation from the original Greek entitled *Iadgari*.

In the Latin West, such a book was called an *antiphonale*, the earliest surviving copies, from Milan and Rome, date from the eighth century.

Latin antiphonalia surviving from the early tenth century (and Greek manuscripts from a somewhat later time) are fully supplied with musical notation for melodies. At first, the notation signs, or *neumes*, indicated only the general direction of melodic movement up or down; they served mainly to assist the memories of singers, who were well trained in the chant tradition. By the eleventh and the thirteenth centuries, both Western and Eastern notation systems began to indicate exact pitch, but this development was shown in different ways.

In the West, it meant the invention of the staff, which is still the basis of Western pitch notation today. The Byzantine East opted for a "digital" system, in which each sign indicated a specific diatonic interval, higher or lower than the pitch of the preceding sign. This system was simplified and modernized in the early nineteenth century.

Eventually, the traditions of the most important centers began to overwhelm, replace, or merge with those of the smaller and less powerful.

Among Greek-speaking Orthodox Christians, the two strongest traditions—the Divine Liturgy of Constantinople's cathedral (Hagia Sophia) and the monastic liturgy of Palestine—gradually merged to form what we know as the Byzantine rite. It absorbed or supplanted the smaller, more local traditions of Antioch, Jerusalem, Alexandria, and southern Italy. This hybrid Byzantine liturgy was carried by Greek Orthodox missionaries into the Slavic world, where it survives today in the Bulgarian, Russian, LTU Rusin, Serbian, Ukrainian, and Rumanian chant traditions.

Some Eastern Christians who spoke languages other than Greek, and held theological views unacceptable to Rome or Constantinople, managed to hold onto their own traditions. The Armenian church, for instance, which derived its liturgies from the pre-Byzantine worship of Jerusalem, retained its independence. Unfortunately, many Armenian medieval manuscripts contain musical notation that cannot now be deciphered. Like the Greek, Armenian notation was modernized in the early nineteenth century.

Syriac-speaking Christians preserved much material from Jerusalem and Antioch lost to the Greek Orthodox. The east Syrian or Assyrian Orthodox (Nestorian) Church, situated within the Persian Empire in Mesopotamia, possessed the only litur-

> Regardless of personal religious beliefs, people need a stable peacefulness to focus upon or life becomes unbearable. For some, that peace comes from listening to the love songs of a humpback whale. For others, Gregorian chant fills the need. Music and sound patterns have well-documented effects (positive and negative) upon the human psyche, and Gregorian chants reverberate with a sense of peace and spiritual connection that is sorely lacking in our current culture.
>
> **Greg O'Bergin**
> COMPUTER PROGRAMMER

gical tradition that developed outside the Hellenized world (a Nestorian group that united with Rome in the sixteenth century is known as the Chaldean church). During the Middle Ages the Assyrian tradition was brought all the way to China and India by Nestorian missionaries; a Catholic branch, known as the Malabar rite, survives in India. (In more recent times a branch of the west Syrian, or Syrian Orthodox Church, has been established in India. Part of it has entered communion with Rome and is known as the Malankar rite.)

The Maronites of Lebanon, united with Rome since the Crusades, preserve an independent liturgy closely related to the Syrian traditions. Neither of these traditions ever adopted written musical notation, and their melodies are transmitted orally to this day.

GREGORIAN CHANT

In the Latin-speaking West, the Roman Catholic Gregorian chant tradition ultimately prevailed, a synthesis of Roman and Frankish liturgies. The earliest surviving manuscripts of Gregorian chant (eighth to tenth centuries) date from the period when a standardized liturgy was being assembled and imposed on all the churches in the domain ruled by Charlemagne (c.742–814) and his successors.

In the late sixth century Pope Gregory the Great (reigned 590–604) had begun an effort to collect Christendom's chant music, and the prestige of Gregory's name was attached to the later organizing effort. Thus, the medieval belief that the "Gregorian" repertory was Roman assured its eventual hegemony over most of the other Western local traditions.

These traditions included the Gallican chant of France, the Beneventan of southern Italy, the northern Italian traditions of Ravenna and Aquilea, and the Mozarabic rite of Spain. (The Mozarabic rite has been permitted to survive in one chapel of the Toledo cathedral.) By the thirteenth century,

Gregorian chant had entered even the ancient Roman basilicas and supplanted the Old Roman chant Only the local chant of Milan, called Ambrosian chant because it was alleged to have been created by St. Ambrose, managed to survive into the twentieth century.

NEW MEDIEVAL DEVELOPMENTS

Once the basic Byzantine and Gregorian repertories were formed, musicians began to standardize and improve the teaching and performance of chant. In both the Eastern and Western churches, there began the adoption of a system of chant modes, coupled with a developing system of notation. These advances were in turn refined by the creation of a new literature of music, one that adapted concepts from classical Greek music theory to such considerations as the phenomena of the range and tuning of pitches and the characteristics of the modes. This development went furthest in the West, spurred by the reconsideration of books on music theory by writers such as Boethius (c.480–524) and Isidore of Seville (c.560–636).

The culmination of the process could be said to be the invention of the staff, more or less as we know it today, by that most important of medieval Western musical theorists, Guido of Arezzo (d. after 1033). He is also credited with organizing the solmization system that developed into our "Do, Re, Mi."

In many regions, particularly in the Carolinian Empire, England, and northern Italy, new types of music and texts were being created to decorate and expand the older repertory. Whereas the texts of Gregorian chant were frequently excerpts and paraphrases from the Bible, the new texts were more often poetic or literary, full of biblical allusions but not extracted from any single biblical passage. Much of the new music was monophonic, a single vocal line of great sophistication and beauty, but in a style different from the older Gregorian melodies. And, too, some of the new music was polyphonic, consisting of one or more additional harmonizing melodies to be sung simultaneously with the chant.

When during the Mass would chants be sung? From the testimony of ninth- and tenth-century writers such as Amalarius of Metz (c. 780–851), decorative, untexted melodies (neumae) were often sung following the gospel antiphons and at the close of the alleluia of the Mass, where they were called *jubili*. Neumae would also be sung at lauds and vespers services. The *trope*, another of the chant modes, accompanied the introit, offertory, and communion.

The most important single addition to the Gregorian repertory, the chant mode known as sequences, or *proses*, constitutes a liturgical genre in its own right, with a history extending for several centuries. By the end of the ninth century, sequences were composed as independent pieces both east and west of the Rhine, as well as in Italy and England. They are commonly made up of prose couplets of varying lengths, with different music for each successive couplet of text. It was a common practice to quote from a particular alleluia melody at the opening of the sequence melody, thereby referring to the historical connection between alleluia and sequence.

The liturgical texts and music created to expand upon the Gregorian repertory constitute the most important music composed in northern Europe during the centuries immediately following the Carolinian Renaissance. It was within these repertories that specific regions (and even individual religious institutions) customized their liturgical practices and preserved vestiges of the traditions displaced by the Gregorian repertory.

During this same period (ninth to eleventh centuries), new monophonic melodies continued to be generated in the older musical genres of Gregorian chant, and for the first time they began to be written down in a kind of book known as the *Kyriale*. This was also a time of great expansion of the office, with new texts and music being composed in abundance for the hundreds of new saints added to the calendars of various regions and centers.

Organum, the practice of performing Gregorian chant polyphonically, usually with improvised harmonizing parts, is described as early as the tenth century. The most important polyphony (different melodic lines performed simultaneously) to survive from before the early twelfth century is saved in manuscripts from Winchester (c. 1000) and Chartres (late eleventh century).

WESTERN LITURGICAL CHANT:
TWELFTH AND THIRTEENTH CENTURIES

The energetic reforms of Christendom during the eleventh, twelfth, and thirteenth centuries had their musical parallel in a reconsideration of Gregorian chant, led by newly formed religious orders, especially the Cistercians and the Augustinian canons regular. While the Augustinians usually followed most of the liturgical traditions of the diocese in which their house was located, everywhere they went they led the way in the development of a new style of sequence. The text of these new sequences were written in accented rhythmic poetry, and this change in poetic style affected musical style as well. Many sequences were designed so that each textual unit, be it phrase, line, or strophe, had its own sharply marked group of notes, to the end that the structure of the music perfectly reflected the text.

The best known of all liturgical and musical reforms of the twelfth to the thirteenth centuries are those of the Cistercians, an order of reformed Benedictine monks. The Cistercians attempted to return to a strict interpretation of the Benedictine rule. Thus they sought a music that reflected their understanding of what liturgical practice had been in Benedict's time, the sixth century. They studied chant from the city of Metz (believed to be the purest dialect of Gregorian chant) and the hymns of St. Ambrose as preserved in the Milanese tradition. The result was a chant stripped of long melismatic passages and often reworked to fit their new understanding, yet remaining essentially Gregorian.

In both cathedral and monastery, the new music written for the mass and office during this period reflected that increasing devotion to the Virgin Mary being felt throughout Europe. There was a great number of new feasts in her honor, and previously existing marian feasts were elevated to higher rank. The new and greater feasts required new and special texts and music, accounting for the great number of marian sequences and hymns retained from these two centuries.

POLYPHONY OF THE TWELFTH AND THIRTEENTH CENTURIES

In the twelfth and thirteenth centuries a difference developed between the polyphonic repertory of northern Europe and that of France, especially of Aquitane in the south of France. It was a difference that would come to play an important role in the development of Western music.

Instead of the added voice being closely tied to the original chant, with one or a few notes for each note of the chant melody, the added voice in the Aquitanian florid style of polyphony was freer, consisting in an elaborate countermelody. The added polyphonic voice was often the more active voice, providing a group of notes for each individual pitch of the original chant. As a result, the chant melody came to be sung more slowly, in notes that were held a relatively long time.

The most important liturgical polyphony of northern France during this period

> Gregorian chant has always invoked in me a deep sense of the Medieval world, its mysteries, and its sense of isolation. I have used it many times in my productions of Shakespeare's English history plays. I have always found this liturgical music, along with Shakespeare's great poetry, to be haunting and meditative.
>
> **James Dunn**
> DIRECTOR, ACTOR
> PROFESSOR EMERITUS, COLLEGE
> OF MARIN DRAMA
> DEPARTMENT

was apparently composed for the cathedral of Notre Dame in Paris. Parisian composers (and subsequently the theorists and notators who preserved their music) began to organize polyphony into rhythmic patterns, slowly replacing a practice that had hitherto been rhythmically unpatterened. By the mid-thirteenth century, a liturgical polyphony existed that was expressed in rhythmic notation, so that, for the first time in the history of Western music, duration was indicated precisely. In this system long and short notes were organized into ternary patterns called *rhythmic modes*. Music notation that relies on these patterns is called *modal notation*.

It is well to remember that, although polyphonic repertories were the most innovative musical repertories created during this time, they would not have been performed in the monasteries or in the more northern European cathedrals. Throughout the Middle Ages and the Renaissance, Gregorian chant and sequences prevailed throughout Europe as the common repertory of liturgical music.

THE LATE MIDDLE AGES AND RENAISSANCE

With the rise of the patronage system in the West, beginning in the fourteenth century, the social context for music-making began to change dramatically. Leadership in musical creativity passed to a new kind of institution: the private court chapel of wealthy noblemen or high-ranking ecclesiastics, such as a cardinal or the pope. Musically trained clerics, the most expert to be found, would staff the private chapel and perform music at the court. Each musician would be paid by means of one or more benefices—that is, appointment to a well-paying ecclesiastical post, such as bishop or abbot. Though an obvious abuse, this practice did make possible the rise of the highly trained, specialized musical professional and the vast repertories of exquisite music that such musicians composed and performed.

The music of the fourteenth century was described by its practitioners as a "new art" (*Ars Nova*), and earlier polyphonic compositions were relegated to *Ars Antiqua*.

Characteristics of the new art included hocket ("hiccup"), in which two or more singers alternate notes and rests, and notation that permitted each beat to be subdivided into two equal smaller notes as well as the traditional three, paving the way for the development of duple meters. Although Pope John XXII, in a famous bull of 1322, forbade the use of most of these techniques in church music, his wishes were completely ignored.

What appears to be the first polyphonic setting of the complete mass by a single person is *La Messe de Nostre Dame* by the most important composer of fourteenth-century France, Guillaume de Machaut (d. 1377), a canon of Reims cathedral who held posts at several royal courts.

In the early fifteenth century musical leadership shifted to English composers, led by Leonel Power (d.1445) and John Dunstaple (d.1453). The new English style was admired on the continent for its avoidance of dissonance and its frequent use of the intervals of the third and the sixth. These English composers also developed the *cantus firmus* mass, the first fully unified settings of the entire mass ordinary, achieved by basing all the movements on the same tenor melody, often a Gregorian chant or a secular song. From this time on, the five movement ordinary (Kyrie, Gloria, Credo, Sanctus, Agnus Dei) became the most important sacred musical form in the West. Several writers of the period regarded the new English style as a new beginning in music history, and for music historians today the period still marks the end of the Middle Ages and the beginning of the Renaissance.

The greatest composer of the Renaissance, Josquin Des Prez (d.1521), belonged to a generation with exceptional musical talent. Their use of imitative counterpoint and other techniques enabled them to treat all the polyphonic voices equally and gave them unprecedented control over their material. As Martin Luther remarked in his *Table Talk*, Josquin was a "master of the notes. They must do as he wills." In his motets, Josquin revealed a special interest in the expressive possibilities of an unusually broad range of texts, exploring an area that would increasingly interest composers for the rest of the sixteenth century.

This new emphasis on the text had a number of interrelated historical causes: Renaissance interest in literature and poetry, the greater availability of books due to the invention of printing, and the Reformation's controversies over the Bible and religious writings. The musical directives issued during and after the Council of Trent emphasized, as the two most important charac-

When I was first exposed to Gregorian chant, I loved its simplicity and equanimity, but I did not fully appreciate the difficulties of creating such a thing until, at the suggestion of my Spiritual Master, Adi Da, I tried composing some chants myself. I soon learned that "skill" was a secondary issue, that art in the service of the Divine required a lot of the Divine and not so much of myself. It even seems to me now that all true art—art that points toward liberation and assists ecstasy—is necessarily sacred art.

Ray Lynch
MUSICIAN, COMPOSER
TWICE BILLBOARD'S NEW AGE
ARTIST OF THE YEAR

teristics of sacred music, the intelligibility of texts and the elimination of secular elements. These directives led to a number of experiments by composers attempting to minimize the florid passages and the simultaneous singing of different syllables in different parts of liturgical song.

The most famous experiment of this kind, the *Missa Papae Marcelli* of the Roman composer Giovanni Pierluigi da Palestrina (1525–1594), became the object of a romantic legend that Palestrina had it performed at the Council of Trent itself, averting at the eleventh hour a determined attempt by the assembled bishops to ban all polyphony from the Catholic liturgy. Another legend, one that is more certainly mere legend, concerns the so-called instrument-free vocal *a capella* attributed to Renaissance music. Except in the pope's private chapel and perhaps a few other places, instruments were commonly used to accompany vocal polyphony in church. We still know less than we should about the liturgical practices that created late medieval and Renaissance music.

THE LEGACY OF MEDIEVAL AND RENAISSANCE MUSIC TODAY

Most of the Eastern churches continued to cling to their monophonic chant, as most do to this day. The first to make extensive use of polyphonic music was the Russian Orthodox church, influenced first by German Lutheran chorales and then by Italian operatic music. The Russian Orthodox also utilized a modified staff notation introduced from the West. In the Armenian Orthodox church, polyphony has been sung since at least the nineteenth century. The Greek Orthodox churches, in the early nineteenth century, modernized their medieval neumatic notation.

In the West, the concern for textual declamation and emotional expression ultimately brought Renaissance polyphony to an end, leading to the development of opera and the new Baroque style. For a long time, however, Renaissance music continued to be performed in churches.

The nineteenth century saw the beginning of a great revival of both medieval chant (particularly by the Benedictines of the Abbey of Solesmes) and Renaissance polyphony. This "Early Music" revival continued into the twentieth century, when it was greatly helped by the new availability of recordings.

> Chant is the grassroots of the Western musical tradition, a primordial outpouring of the most beautiful melodies ever conceived. Every period of composition has drawn inspiration from chant, but none more so than the Renaissance, whose polyphonists founded their whole art and technique on it.
>
> **Peter Phillips**
> MUSICIAN, MUSICOLOGIST
> DIRECTOR, THE TALLIS SCHOLARS

The ideals of the nineteenth century were enshrined in Pope Pius X's *Tra le sollecitudini* of 1903, often described as the charter of the liturgical movement. In this document, the pope taught that Gregorian chant was the supreme model of liturgical music and that Renaissance polyphony came closest to it in spirit. After Vatican II, however, the disappearance of Latin and the new openness to folk and popular music led to a general abandonment of Gregorian chant and to a polarization between those church musicians who wished to preserve chant, polyphony, and classical music, and those who thought it more important to promote popular music in the renewed liturgy. After a quarter-century standoff, it is time to move to a new synthesis.

Chant and polyphony will not go away. In fact, they are more popular among the general public than they have been for centuries. Just as the church can never abandon its Judaic, Greek, and Latin heritage, it can never forget its historic musical heritage, an extraordinary treasury of profound musical wisdom. Chant and liturgy developed together as a single organic growth; chant music is imbued with the spirit of centuries of religious feeling and thought. The polyphony that developed out of Gregorian chant partake of this spirit. And just as theology today cannot ignore the historical development of doctrine from the early church to the present, so our musical life will not be healthy if it is expected to operate in a historical vacuum cut off from the past. The continued study and performance of this treasury of sacred music, the ancient and venerable ancestor of many of the kinds of music we enjoy today, is essential, and would have the beneficial side-effect of dramatically improving the standard expected of all the other kinds of music performed in modern worship. ∎

A Choirboy's Life in the Middle Ages

by Robert Winter

Many of the plainchants and early polyphony were sung neither by men nor women but by young boys. The church fathers found scriptural justification for this practice in Psalm 8, which speaks of "Thou whose glory above the heavens is chanted by the mouth of babes and infants." The sweet, clear sounds of young voices added a tone of purity and innocence to the worship services. Moreover, the choirboys provided a pool from which future clerics could be drawn.

The Cathedral of Notre Dame at Paris maintained about eight choirboys during the golden period of Notre Dame organum. A few of the boys were either poor orphans or sons of noblemen, though most of them came from artisan or merchant families in and around Paris. Boys were generally admitted at the age of eight, at which time they had to pass a musical audition and demonstrate evidence of a religious disposition. The parents were required to sign an irrevocable contract of six to ten years' duration, during which time the child could not be removed.

At the beginning of the fifteenth century, Jean Gerson, a theologian, published a *Doctrina*, or plan, for the education and governance of the choirboys at the cathedral. Gerson's book, from which these excerpts are drawn, is presumed to describe practices from the twelfth and thirteenth centuries as well.

(1) Above all, the master should be the most upright person, because...the pupil will do nothing except that which he sees the master doing....

(2) Moreover, let him frequently exhort the love of God...because in and through the divine service they may ascend to Paradise and escape the cruel torments of Hell.

(3) In addition, they are to be led to confession not just once a year, but four or six times....And there should be an appropriate confessor instituted for them, because more

prudence is often required in confessing well with them than with older people, so that they should not be examined too little or too much.

(5) Moreover, the master of music shall teach the boys at the statutory hours primarily plainchant and counterpoint...but no dissolute or ribald songs.

(6) Likewise, we wish that one of the boys should always read during every meal from some useful book so that they might abstain from conversation and observe that admonition "to speak few things during a meal."

(8) Likewise, each boy should inform on his comrade concerning the following things: if he has heard him speak French; if he has sworn; if he has uttered a lie or other falsehood; if he has said injurious things; if he has struck anyone; if he has risen too late; if he has babbled in church and done similar things. And if he has not accused the wrongdoer, he himself, for him and with him, is to be similarly punished.

(9) Moreover, all games are prohibited that lead to avarice, indecency, immodest noise, anger, or rancor, such as games of dice or chance....Yet frequent and brief periods of recreation are to be given the boys, as for example shortly after the noon meal and after dinner, which times are of little use for other serious things.

(10) And let one master always be present.

(11) Moreover, we do not want the boys to go to any place or dwelling or church to sing unless by special license of the superiors. And then the master should be present to see that they do not indulge in too much food or otherwise behave themselves immodestly.

(15) They are to be prohibited from consuming too much food and drink in the morning and at other times, through which the preservation of their voices may be hindered.

(16) In addition, in the choir they must sit apart from each other and not talk among themselves....And they should especially serve in silence and with appropriate decorum near the altar when the sacred mysteries of the Mass are celebrated, without laughing, chattering, or making noises or indecent gestures among themselves or with others, but should serve just like Angels of God, so that all who see them might say: "These are truly angelic boys and such as the Immaculate Virgin ought to have in her church, the most renowned in all the world." ■

2

Serenity in Song

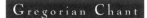

Sacred Sound, Sacred Song

CHANT IN FIVE RELIGIOUS TRADITIONS

by Timothy Rayborn

HE MARRIAGE OF *sacred words to the human voice is a crucial aspect of worship in nearly all of the world's faiths. Just as there is no known culture without religion, there is no great religion without sacred music expressed through the voice of a chanter.*

Each tradition approaches its chant in a different manner, but all assert that the words and sounds have an intrinsic holiness representative of a higher reality. Hindus, for example, believe that the chanting of Vedic hymns brings one into harmony with the vibratory patterns of the cosmos. Tibetan Buddhists use chant as meditation and to communicate with the spirit world. Synagogue chant expresses Jewish belief in the close connection between God and humanity. Early Medieval Christians, drawing upon Hellenistic philosophy, came to view chant as an audible expression of God's perfect creation. To Islam, chanting of the Holy Qur'an is "the art of sound," superior to mere music.

HINDUISM

From the earliest age, the belief that sound is sacred formed the base of Hindu mystical and philosophical systems.

The concept of sacred sound is at the very heart of the Vedas (Sanskrit *vid*, "to know"), a term generally applied to four collections of hymns and sacrificial formulas brought to India by Aryans settling the Indus valley region about 1500 BC. Already ancient at this time, the Vedas were considered eternal, not produced by human agency. Their authors had merely "seen" or discovered these hymns and chants, and thus were known as *rsis*, or seers.

So holy are the texts that the very act of hearing this divine wisdom is considered sacred and the slightest error in the priests' reciting or chanting could bring disaster. Tales of a single mispronounced syllable causing ruin to kingdoms and madness to the singer-priest are legend.

The *Rgveda*, the oldest collection, consists of 1,028 hymns to Vedic gods. To protect the magical qualities of the words, mathematical formulae were devised to reorder, add, and repeat syllables, words, phrases, and even verses. As the need for a written text of the Vedas became apparent, a simple system of three accents was devised to indicate the general flow of the melody. *Rgveda* chants are thus generally limited to a range of three notes.

The melodic range of the *Samaveda* is considerably larger, often encompassing a whole octave. The *Yajurveda*, by contrast, employs what is perhaps the simplest of all Vedic chanting, using speech tone without pitch variation. The *Arthavaveda*, the last of the four, is essentially a collection of magical formulae, charms, spells, incantations, and hymns of philosophical speculation.

The importance of the Vedic philosophy of sound to Hindu chanting cannot be exaggerated. Vedic philosophy posits the concept of *nada brahma* ("sound god") as the source of all vibration, audible or inaudible, in the cosmos. Manifested sound, or *ahatananda*, is dependent upon its counterpart, *anahatananda*, or unmanifested sound. The latter is seen as the creative principle of the universe and is iconographically represented by *Siva Nataraja*, the "royal dancer" whose right hand holds a drum that vibrates the cosmos into existence. Vedic rituals were meant to bring worshippers into alignment with these divine vibrations and the obvious means was music, preferably chanted vocal music.

In Hinduism, vocal music is understood to be the product of *prana*, or "life-breath." *Prana* passes through the body's *chakras*, or power centers, two of which are particularly important in the production of musical sound. The *anahatchakra*, being in the heart, gives sound its meaning and efficacy, for it is in the heart that the creative principle of *anahatananda* also dwells. The *visuddhachakra* in the throat gives speech and song their audible forms and so allows for the communication of divine truth.

At the center of Vedic expression is the *mantra*, or "sacred utterance." Derived from the root word *man*, or "think," a *mantra* is a "vehicle of thought" that requires concentration upon it by the chanter. *Mantras* may consist of a syllable, word, phrase, or a long and detailed hymn. Repetition of the sound of the *mantra* and concentration upon it place the believer in touch with the higher reality from which the sacred sound first emanated.

The *mantra* par excellence that is chanted and meditated upon by all Hindus is "the first syllable" OM, the eternally creative divine word. OM is also designated as *pranava* ("to utter a droning"), referring to the practice of chanting OM before and after recitations and prayers. Hindus have remarked that in this sense OM is very similar to the *amen* of the Judeo-Christian and Muslim traditions, the sound of which it strongly resembles.

To chant OM, then, affirms for the Hindu that sound is a direct link between humanity and the divine. This is the theme of the entire Veda. The verses are not meant to be read as literature but to be chanted. The chanter, by receiving a share of the cosmic energy, shares in the vibratory process of all creation. The human community is thus renewed via participation in the energy of the Divine.

> In Gregorian chant I see the grandeur of epic, I taste the sweetness of lyric, I sense the majestic awe of the mystery of the Sacrament.
>
> **Robert D. Sider**
> AUTHOR, TEACHER
> PROFESSOR OF CLASSICAL
> LANGUAGES, DICKINSON
> COLLEGE, PENNSYLVANIA

TIBETAN BUDDHISM

The term "Buddhist music" encompasses the variety of vocal and instrumental music of the many Asian peoples who have influenced Buddhism. A look at Tibetan Buddhist chant connects us to a particularly rich musical heritage that is still representative of the larger field.

According to the Theravada tradition of Buddhism, Buddha is said to have deemphasized ritual music, dismissing it as one of the "Ten Fetters" that bind us to worldly existence. Despite this, a tradition of Buddhist chant did arise, influenced by the Vedic chant of Hinduism. In both there are similar rhythms and ranges of musical scales, as well as a shared philosophy about the mystical nature of sound.

Buddhist chanting is not a form of worship in the Western sense, but rather a way of reciting doctrine. Early chants consisted of words believed to have been spoken by the Buddha, hymns of praise to the Buddha, and *mantras* (recited meditations). In the Theravada school of Buddhism, which emphasizes reciting texts, the language of chanting has remained Pali, while the Mahayana school has embraced a more ritualistic, mystical, and musically elaborate form of chanting, adopting the vernacular of each country.

Buddhism was introduced to Tibet during the reign of King Strongtsam Gompo (613–651 AD), whose two wives were Buddhists from China and Nepal, respectively. In that same century, a form of Tantric Mahayana Buddhism, strongly influenced by the Indian cult of Shiva, also entered Tibet and began to combine with the native shamanistic religion of Bon.

> Chant seems to
> help my breathing.
> With Gregorian
> chant I enter into a
> state of non-grief
> melancholy,
> something like awe,
> something like
> sharing in the
> eternal.
>
> **Herbert Gold**
> NOVELIST
> AUTHOR OF FATHERS AND
> A GIRL OF FORTY

Bon ritualism, which sought communion with and appeasement of the supernatural world, had reached a highly elaborate state. While chanting and drumming, a Bon priest would glide, whistle, shout, and mask the voice by raising or lowering pitch. Some of the sounds created were said to represent the voices of spirits heard through the singer as medium.

By the beginning of the tenth century, when the first Buddhist monasteries were founded in Tibet, the religious significance of Bon chant had been adapted to the philosophical and spiritual goals of Tantric Buddhism, and a new form of religious music was born.

Five times daily Tibetan Buddhist monks gather to chant hymns of praise to Buddha or invite benevolent deities to visit their places of worship and meditation. Most commonly, the chant is choral, accompanied by drums, bells, gongs, and flutes.

The service often begins with an instrumental prelude. The monks sit in rows across from each other, led by a director of chant.

The melodic passages of the chant are very carefully and beautifully notated in inks of different colors. Deviations from these notations are theoretically not allowed. The texts are chanted in unison, although occasionally a solo effect will occur, a slight variation in the line by one or more of the singers.

One reason for the occurrence of variations in the line of the chant is the influence of North Indian Hindu ragas. Of course, variations from performance to performance are not necessarily intentional. Some are merely the result of the passage of time. Despite these alterations, the monks' prevailing belief is that the chant has remained unchanged over time.

The soloing effects occur most often in chants known as *dbyans*, or *abyans*. These are long-sustained chants sung in extremely low register, dynamically marked by changes in volume and pitch as the chant progresses.

Two other forms of chant are the *'don*, a form of solo recitation often serving as an introductory passage to a larger work, and the *rta*, melodic choral chants accompanied by drum and cymbal. All three forms, along with instrumental music, are used in monastic ritual.

Two monasteries of the *Dge-lugs-pa* order have produced a special chanting technique, to which the Editor of this book, Huston Smith, alludes in his Introduction, and

which was unknown to the West until Smith discovered it in 1994. This is the monks' ability to achieve mixtures of overtones in their voices, allowing each to sing two or more notes simultaneously. These are most often at the third, two octaves above the intoned note, or the fifth, an octave below. Western science has remained mystified as to how exactly this is accomplished. The explanation put forth by Tibetan Buddhists derives from Bon chant practices: that some of the sounds are those of spirits speaking through the chanters.

The religious goals of Bon Shamanism (communion with and appeasement of the spirit world) and Buddhism (the transformation of consciousness and the realization of enlightenment) have been seamlessly blended in Tibetan monastic chants to produce a liturgical music that is unique in the Buddhist world.

JUDAISM

The music of the Hebrews dates at least from the second millennium BC, but the practice of true biblical chanting seems to have originated in the fifth century BC.

During this period, following the Babylonian Exile, music for services in the Second Temple had become an increasingly elaborate mixture of voices and instruments. Among the instruments were the *kinnor* (lyre), *hatsotserot* (trumpet), *nebel* (harp), *tof* (drums), and *shofar* (the ram's horn to call the faithful to service). The musical duties fell to those who had descended from the tribe of Levi, for King David had appointed the Levites as the Temple musicians.

By the second century BC a growing opposition to the Temple's musical activities had developed, led by the Pharisees, who saw in the rituals of the Temple too much that reminded them of Hellenism. They associated musical instruments and Greek musical scales with drunken revels and worship of multiple gods. When the Temple was destroyed these rabbis assumed the whole responsibility for conducting religious services. They excluded all instrumental music, retaining only the *shofar* to call worshipers to the synagogue. They also moved away from the hierarchical, sacrificial cult of the Temple toward a simpler, more egalitarian form of religious service.

This new synagogue service dispensed with the chorus of Levite singers and instead elected a lay choir director who was responsible for the synagogue chants. To recite scripture without chants was considered a minor sacrilege.

As the Jews spread ever further on both sides of the Mediterranean, Hebrew ceased to be a living language. To safeguard the proper pronunciation, phrasing, and melodies of biblical Hebrew, a system of scriptural notation was developed consisting of accent marks or letters written above or below the texts to indicate the general patterns for chanting. This method of cantillation was completed and accepted by the dispersed Jews during the tenth century and has remained the method of cantillation down to the present age.

These notations do not indicate musical intervals or pitches as notes written on a staff do. Rather they are slashes and signs that point the direction of the musical line, serving as memory aids for the melodies being chanted. This approach created a uniquely "Jewish" style of cantillation that served the dispersed communities well. For even though musical styles differed from region to region, the system preserved the Hebrew biblical tradition of chant.

Beginning in the sixth century, as a unified system for biblical chant was being created, a new form of metrical hymn, the *piyyut*, arose among the *Sephardic* Jews of Spain. These hymns were enriched, after the Islamic conquest of Spain in the eighth century, by ornate and mellifluous Qur'anic chants, which themselves had been influenced by eastern Jewish chants.

The intricacies of this new style necessitated professional singers who could devote themselves to studying new texts and tunes. It is said that the movement rose to brilliant artistic heights, stylistically characterized by improvised song, coloratura and ornately embellished passages, and vocal gymnastics. Improvisation merged with traditional cantillation, resulting in freely created cantorial melodies. Such ornamentation was clearly influenced by Islamic practices, and indeed, some Orthodox thinkers opposed it, most notably Moses Maimonides. But *piyyutim* spread from Spain to other Jewish centers and enjoyed popularity up to the twentieth century.

Another important movement in the history of Jewish chant originated in eighteenth century Poland and Russia, the *chassadic*. The *Chassadim* believed direct communication with God could be achieved through music, especially wordless chants. These *niggunim* (chassidic song), influenced by cabalistic mysticism, often arose spontaneously and had, it was believed, more power than any other prayer, representing pure religious ecstasy. Their melodies derived from both sacred and secular sources.

Today the various Jewish Orthodox sects continue using chants handed down over the centuries. Faithful to the tradition of Ezra, they maintain that the Bible must be chanted, not merely read like speech.

Jewish chant expresses the idea of humanity's closeness to God and God's concern to hear the praises of his human creations. A unique combination of theology, devotion, and music has been created to convey this sense of a close relationship with God. By the shared remembrance of God during chanting, the Jewish community is strengthened and life is affirmed.

CHRISTIANITY

Christianity in its infancy was essentially a sect of Judaism. Common to both was the practice of singing psalms *responsorially*, wherein the congregation sang a response to a soloist, or *antiphonally*, where two groups would sing alternate phrases. Both of these techniques have remained vital aspects of monastic singing to the present day. Innovators in this tradition added harmonies and long-held notes (drones) under the melody, a technique known as *organum*. It was from this that complex polyphonic music developed, one of the glories of the Western "classical" musical tradition.

As Christians began to include Gentiles of the Hellenistic world in their worship, it became natural to make use of Greek in the reading and singing of Hebrew scripture and the New Testament. But the early Church Fathers also reacted against the influence of the Hellene world. They discouraged the use of musical instruments to accompany chant, musical instruments being associated with drunken revels, festivals, and Hellenistic religious practices. While a *kithara* (a harp-like instrument) might be used at family gatherings or lesser rites, the actual Christian liturgy was reserved for the human voice alone.

> I love Gregorian chant. My parents listened to chants and I sort of absorbed them that way. They are suddenly very popular, particularly among kids.
>
> **Mairi McFall**
> LIBRARIAN
> OAKLAND, CALIFORNIA
> PUBLIC LIBRARY SYSTEM

There were even those among early Church Fathers who wanted a prohibition on music altogether. A compromise was reached that accorded with the Neoplatonic philosophy adopted by many Hellenistic Christians: Chant would be encouraged, but only diatonic modes were permitted, that is to say only those modes that corresponded with, to use a modern example, the white notes on a piano keyboard. Sharps and flats were forbidden. Polyphony was initially not permitted and musical instruments were banned. Dancing, hand-clapping, or other rhythmic expressions were also forbidden, owing to their prevalence among Eastern mystery religions and Gnostics.

The use of Greek declined in Rome in the third century, eventually to be replaced by Latin. As the two languages drifted apart, and the Eastern Orthodox and Western Churches separated, different musical traditions developed. Today, only a few Greek words, such as *Kyrie Elieson* ("Lord have mercy"), remain in the chanted Western liturgy.

With the issuing of the Edict of Milan in 313, the Church was able to come out of hiding and turn its attention to the organization of liturgical matters. The construction

of ornate basilicas were begun and it seems likely that the creation of acoustically sound places of worship encouraged the flowering of chant as an art form.

St. Basil, a contemporary of Jerome and Augustine, observed that since the Word of God is a remedy for the sickness of the soul, it is good that a way exists to help with the "ingestion" of that remedy, namely the use of chanting and music, which bring delight to the ear and increase to our understanding and holiness. This was indeed a different philosophy than that advocated by the earlier Fathers—that musical sound was to be severely subservient to the words at all times.

The sixth century saw the beginning of a phenomenal re-emergence of Greek influence on Western music, due in large part to one book, *De institutione musica*, by Anicius Boethius (c.480–524). Essentially a translation into Latin of Pythagorean musical theory, it illustrated Boethius' belief that "music is number made audible." This idea became the cornerstone of European musical theory for well over one thousand years.

Pythagoras taught that all things of beauty are dependent upon the rationality of numbers. He also showed that there is a numerical relationship between the octave fourth, fifth, and unison. Subsequently, medieval theorists considered these four intervals to be the most "perfect" and consonant, due to the simplicity of their numerical ratios. Interestingly, the second was held to be more "pure" than the third, and it thus developed a prominent place in medieval chant, producing a most unusual harmony to modern ears.

Boethius applied the Pythagorean philosophy to Christian thought with the intention of showing how music related to God, the most beautiful of all things. He felt that an aspect of the supreme beauty of God was expressed by the perfection of audible numerical ratios in music. Thus, music was seen as a means of gaining some understanding of the divine.

In Boethius' thought, as well as the theology of music subscribed to by the Medieval Christian Church, *musica instrumentalis* (that which is audible, both voice and instrument) was at the bottom of a musical hierarchy, preceded by *musica humana*, or the mathematically proportioned relationship between body and soul, and culminating in *musica mundana*, or the music of the spheres, that which emanates from the heavenly host and is the foundation of existence. These classifications would remain an integral part of musical theory and philosophy until the Renaissance.

In *musica instrumentalis* the voice is given preference over instruments, as it is the "natural" instrument bestowed upon humanity by God. As a result, musical instruments tended to be regarded with some hostility, especially by the Church. Nevertheless, their use flourished among secular musicians, and some instruments, such as the organ, found their way into Church use.

One of the greater influences of Boethius' thought on Western music was its emphasis on close structural analysis and the theoretical study of music. It was held that if the mathematical order of music be fully appreciated, the listener would derive an intellectual satisfaction not known to the untrained ear.

The name of Pope Gregory I (590–604) enters the picture about 65 years after the death of Boethius. No universally accepted notational system yet existed for Christian chant, and an effort arose during his reign to collect and unify the various sets of chants for the whole of Christendom.

The actual connection between the chant melodies of Gregory's time and the "Gregorian chant," which became the supreme sacred music of the Roman Catholic Church, is unknown. Centuries of oral transmission between the sixth century and the beginning of Christian chant notation in the ninth and tenth centuries prevent certain knowledge of how similar were the chants heard by Gregory to those that bear his name.

With Boethius' death *De institutione musica* fell into disuse, to be rediscovered by scholastics during the ninth-century Carolinian Renaissance. The book subsequently became the most widely used theoretical work on music in the medieval period. Music was studied as a science as much as an art. The chant repertory was cataloged according to its tones, and some chants were altered to be brought more in line with Boethian theory. While the final formats for the chant of the Mass and the content of the feasts were not achieved until somewhat later, by the eleventh century the synthesis of Hebrew and Greek influences on sacred Christian chant was complete.

Drawing from synagogue chant, folk song, and Greek theory, Christians produced their own means of praising God, a music well integrated with their liturgy. Music was seen as expressing in sound the order of God's creation and, as audible perfection, chant came to be esteemed as a vehicle for transmission of the divine message.

ISLAM

For the Muslim, chanting is inseparable from public life. Five times a day the *mu'adhdin* ("muezzin") chants the call to prayer (*adhan*) from the minaret, varying the lines and the repetitions of words according to the time of the day. A variety of chants are employed during festivals, holidays, and other special events. These include the pilgrim songs of the *hajj* (sung chorally), chants celebrating the Prophet's ascent to heaven (especially marked by the Sufi orders), and the celebrations of the month of Ramadan, when it is the practice in mosques to chant the entire Qur'an.

The history of these chants can be traced back to the time of the Prophet Muhammad, whose public speeches were the primary means by which the Qur'an was

> When we recorded *Mysteria*, our CD of Gregorian chant, I was reminded of my early days in Catholic school, when we sang the Gregorian chant Requiem every Friday morning. I remember how good it felt singing those beautiful melodies. Chant has always conveyed to me a certain mystery that is decidedly special. It symbolizes a spirituality that doesn't need dogma or the Vatican, a spirituality that was always there and will continue to be there.
>
> **Louis Botto**
>
> SINGER, MUSICIAN
> FOUNDER AND ARTISTIC
> DIRECTOR OF CHANTICLEER

transmitted to others. Muhammad is said to have personally given sanction to the practice of *adhan*, instituting it in the first or second year of the Hijra (622–4). The *adhan* was meant to distinguish the Islamic call to prayer from those of Judaism (done with the *shofar*) and Christianity (the ringing of bells).

Rites of passage, such as birth, circumcision, marriage, and death, are frequently commemorated with the use of Qur'anic recitation. Political events may include chant as well. Such occasions usually make use of skilled recitors, who have spent years developing their art. On a daily basis, however, all Muslims engage in some form of recitation, particularly the *salat*, the five daily prayers wherein each Muslim recites *Fatihah*, the opening Surah of the Qur'an.

Chant is not considered *musiqa*, or music, which is forbidden in places of worship because of its secular implications. Instead, it is considered an art form, *handasah al sawt*, or "the art of sound."

Islamic melodies and techniques of chanting have changed little since the seventh century. While there are regional differences, the underlying qualities are always noticeable. The Qur'an's theological ideas are the basis for this.

Since God cannot be associated with any earthly object, including music, no attempt is made to convey the divine through melody; the text alone sufficing, without melodic symbolism.

A related notion is that, as God is infinite, the chant lines should be constructed upon the idea of "infinite" patterns. Through manipulation of pitches and duration, the musical progression seeks to convey an unfolding that never ends.

What one beholds in the floral patterns and calligraphy that adorn the mosque, for example, is a sense of the infinite, without a beginning or end. This is what the "free," nonrhythmic quality of the chant seeks to express as well: Just as the chant does not have rhythmic constraints or a feeling of beginning and ending, so it is like God, upon whom there are no constraints or boundaries.

The effect of infinite patterns in the chant is enhanced, paradoxically, by repetitive musical themes and formulas. Repetition adds to the unending quality that is sought, as the listener cannot be sure when and where a melodic line shall end.

The dynamic character of Islamic chant is rarely achieved through standard musical approaches, such as large-scale thematic development or changes in tempo. Instead, the "excitement" of Qur'anic chant is created through an emphasis on the density of the line itself, i.e., the number of notes in a given section, their placement, and the range of the musical scale.

This labyrinth of tonal and durational progressions is composed of short themes, rather than extended ones, which the skilled singer utilizes with ever increasing complexity, creating dynamic tension.

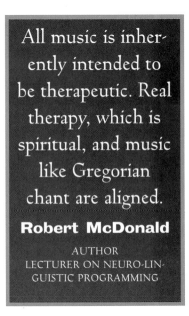

All music is inherently intended to be therapeutic. Real therapy, which is spiritual, and music like Gregorian chant are aligned.

Robert McDonald

AUTHOR
LECTURER ON NEURO-LINGUISTIC PROGRAMMING

Another element in the dynamics of Qur'anic chant is its stress upon the autonomous nature of the individual verse. This might seem at odds with the concept of an infinite work without beginning or end, but in fact it supports the idea. Each segment has its own "life"; the potential for thematic development from opening to conclusion is all but eliminated. While successive segments of chant may grow more complex, they do not build upon each other in a thematic manner. Thus, the chant cannot be reduced to a single theme or movement that serves as a summary for the work as a whole.

A final element is that of intricacy and ornateness in the sung line. Muslims view this characteristic not as decoration, but as the very substance of the melody.

The intended effect of Qur'anic chant is the involvement of the faithful with the emotion and thought of the chant. The audience is meant to take part in the process; no one is a "casual" listener.

Qur'anic chant is thus an interactive phenomenon. While it is deliberately nonrepresentational, it is reflective of Islamic culture as a whole, which seeks to center itself around the divine. It is God's Word to all humanity, manifested in an audible art form, and within its complex structures can be found the mind-set of the Muslim faithful.

CONCLUSION

The value of chant as an art form in and of itself must not be overlooked. While the primacy of the holy words is paramount, particularly to the devout, absolute comprehension of them is not necessary to feel an emotional response. One may be captivated by the serene, haunting quality of a Gregorian chant, inspired by the almost anguished call of the muezzin, or wonder at the multi-tonal dbyan sung by a Buddhist monk, and not understand a word of Latin, Arabic, or Tibetan.

Within these five traditions melody is generally subservient to words, but it is evident that aesthetic appreciation of chant by the faithful is important to chant's appeal, though perhaps less so in the Eastern chants than in the Western. Even so, the faithful Hindus will treasure their mantras just as Jews joyously sing praises to God. Islam, while not recognizing Qur'anic chant as music, nevertheless holds international competitions to reward the most skillful chanters.

Chant reflects both a belief in the power of the transcendent and the human capacity to create works of surpassing excellence. Perhaps what inspires reverence toward the sacred is the same source that gives impetus to the glorification of artistic achievement. While the adherents of these five traditions might argue that the true source of beauty and wonder is the divine, it is nevertheless through the vehicle of the human voice that such qualities are expressed, and that alone is a kind of miracle. ■

Boethius and the Medieval Philosophy of Music

by Timothy Rayborn

In the early sixth century AD, as Germanic tribes demolished the Pax Romana and Romans ceased to be the rulers of their own empire, the Church increasingly felt the need for a reconciliation between Classical and Christian values. The transmission of Greek musical theory to the West that occurred at this time was due in large part to the efforts of one man, Anicius Manilius Severinus Boethius (c.480–524), a Roman statesman in the service of the Ostrogothic King Theodoric. For over 1,000 years, Boethius' achievement would continue to influence philosophers, theologians, and the theorists and composers of Gregorian chant.

Boethius's writings exerted an especially great influence throughout the Middle Ages. His treatise, *De institutione musica*, preserved important Greek theoretical works, particularly of the Pythagorean tradition, and gave the medieval world a theory not only of the structure of music, but, indeed, of all reality.

This work is essentially a translation into Latin from Greek of the lost *De musica* of Nichomacus, and of Ptolemy's *Harmonics*. It is an attempt to include Pythagorean musical theory within a Neoplatonic framework, while giving it a relevance to education by drawing from Aristotle. In the text, Boethius states that, fundamentally, "music is number made audible." This philosophy would be the cornerstone of European musical theory for over a millennium.

Pythagoras had believed that music demonstrates in sound the pure world of number, and derived its beauty from that world. He concluded that all things of beauty (not only number) are dependent upon the rationality of numbers and can be explained by them.

This philosophy was applied to Christian thought by Boethius with the intention of showing how music related to God, the most beautiful of all things. He felt that the supreme beauty of God could also be expressed as a numerical ratio, which corresponded to the audible ratios of music. Thus, music was a means of gaining some understanding of the divine and, as Albert Seay states in his book, *Music in the Medieval World*, "It is here that music achieves its real place in medieval philosophy, for, as a microcosm of the macrocosm, it can duplicate on a small scale the power of number inherent in the otherwise almost incomprehensible grand expanse about us."

Boethius saw music as holding a special place within the liberal arts, which to him were arithmetic, music, geometry, and astronomy. Unlike the other arts, music, he believed, directly related to moral conduct. This notion stemmed from the Neoplatonic tradition that argued for the existence of "good" and "bad" music, both of which could influence impressionable young minds. Platonic philosophy held that good music ennobled the soul and calmed the passions, creating a harmonious individual. Music that was purely for entertainment, by contrast, served only to arouse improper behavior in its listeners and contributed to the downfall of the state.

As a Neoplatonist, as well as a student of Aristotle, Boethius felt it was necessary that music be understood, controlled, and directed so that it might help properly shape the individual. At the end of the first chapter of *De institutione musica*, he writes "From all these accounts it appears without doubt that music is so naturally united with us that we cannot be free from it even if we so desired. For this reason, the power of the intellect ought to be summoned so that this art, innate through nature, might also be mastered and comprehended through knowledge."

This remarkable statement is a summary of his essential philosophy. Here he links music with the very essence of humanity, and, by extension, to God, since all things are a united and ordered system, held together by divinely ordained numerical principles.

In significant contrast to the actual daily aspects of monastic worship, which involved extensive amounts of singing the scriptures (the amount grew over the centuries to reach immense proportions), Boethius held that the key relation to music was in its study, not in music-making itself. Music could indeed be pleasing to the ear, but its prime value was as a science, not an art. The act of distancing oneself from the sound and delving into the theory would ensure that a proper study of music's structure could be undertaken. The beauty of the mathematical order would then be fully appreciated, and when the sounds were actually heard, the listener would derive an intellectual satisfaction not known to the untrained ear.

Boethius defined music as existing on three levels: *musica instrumentalis, musica humana*, and *musica mundana*, classifications that would remain an integral part of musical theory and philosophy in general until the Renaissance. The latter two terms, in fact, have nothing to do with music as we think of it, but were rather expressions of medieval theology and cosmology, drawn from the theories of the ancients.

Musica instrumentalis was seen as the "lowest" type of music, that which was produced by the human voice and musical instruments. Here the voice was given preference because it was the "natural" instrument bestowed upon humanity by God. As a result, musical instruments tended to be regarded with some hostility, especially by the Church. Nevertheless, their use flourished among secular musicians, and some, such as the organ and symphony (also known as the organistrum, an early type of hurdy-gurdy), found their way into Church use.

The primary purpose of *musica instrumentalis*, in this philosophy, was to give an audible representation of the numerical ratios of musical intervals, commonly demonstrated on the single string instrument known as the monochord, which displayed such ratios through the stopping of the string at various points—an early example of the principle upon which all stringed instruments are based.

The next level of music, *musica humana*, referred to both the symmetry of the physical structure of the human body, and the harmony between physical health and the virtues of the immortal soul. Boethius would have certainly concurred with Ptolemy's assertion that the octave, fifth, and fourth have their counterpart in the soul's ability to think, perceive, and learn skills. The relationship of body to soul was believed to be based upon numerical ratios and was therefore a form of "music."

The highest level of music, *musica mundana*, is known today by the romantic and oft-quoted Pythagorean phrase "music of the spheres." For Boethius it was that which was apparent in the orderly passage of time (the years and the seasons), the orderly progression of the heavenly bodies, and the interaction of the four elements. Christians perceived *musica mundana* to be the music chanted by the angels singing the *Sanctus* from the Ordinary of the Mass ("Holy, holy, holy") around the throne of God.

It was in *musica mundana* that the numerical principles had their origin. The two lower levels of *musica* were reflections of the perfect ratios that formed the structure of reality, as created by God. Audible music and the body-soul relationship thus served as examples of the numerical perfection inherent in the divine and in creation.

De institutione musica fell into disuse after Boethius' death but was rediscovered by scholastics during the ninth-century Carolinian Renaissance. It subsequently became the most widely used theoretical work on music in the medieval period. It survives in no less than 137 medieval and Renaissance manuscripts, a testament to its importance. ■

Music of the Hemispheres

A Conversation with Dr. Kenneth R. Pelletier

R. KENNETH R. PELLETIER'S *work in the field of holistic medicine has played a major role in America's present rethinking of health-care practices. The Stanford Corporate Health Program, which he directs, and whose members include IBM, American Airlines, and AT&T, is providing a model for corporate managers of how positive health practices, such as meditation, exercise, a healthy diet, and appropriate medical care, can improve workers' health and reduce the need (and costs) of after-the-fact care. In person, and despite his busy schedule, he conveys the sense of stressless ease that his advocacy of healthy living is meant to bring to others.*

Since 1979, Dr. Pelletier has been the President of the American Health Association. He is a clinical associate professor of medicine at the Stanford University School of Medicine and the author of seven books on wellness and mind/body health, including the now classic best-seller Mind as Healer, Mind as Slayer. *His latest book,* Sound Mind, Sound Body, *was described by Dr. Andrew Weil as "...an excellent demonstration of the first principle of holistic medicine: We are more than just physical bodies." As Dr. Deepak Chopra recently put it, "Dr. Pelletier has redefined health as an expression of higher states of consciousness."*

Dr. Pelletier manages to combine an active outdoor lifestyle with a full schedule of medical and advisory work. An equestrian and avid open-ocean sailor, he lives on a farm in Danville, California, with his wife, Elizabeth, and their thoroughbred horses, Shaughnessy and Sullivan. This interview was scheduled around a trip to Washington, DC, where he was to attend the first meeting of the new Office of Alternative Medicine of the National Institutes of Health.

He comes to his interest in chant naturally. Long before he was a scientist, he was an altar boy at his Catholic parish church in Rhode Island. There, assisting the priest at High Mass, he first heard Gregorian chant.

Do you recall your reaction the first time you heard Gregorian chant?
Pelletier: Yes, I remember it very well. I was probably nine or ten years old, serving at the High Mass. What was my reaction? In a word—tears. I was emotionally moved in a way that even then surprised me. It was completely inexplicable. I felt this combination of joy and sadness, and a lot of paradoxical, simultaneous emotions. I remember it very clearly.

What was wonderful was that, as a boy, I could listen to Gregorian chant live. I was raised a French Catholic at a time when all the Catholic services were in pure Latin. As an altar boy, I always volunteered to serve at the High Mass, where you had the chanting and the incense and the recitation of the liturgy in Latin, because I found those masses to be more moving and more powerful than any of the other services.

I was also fortunate to have an uncle, an attorney in Washington, DC, who considered it part of his nephew's cultural upbringing to have him go to Washington and spend considerable time in the Smithsonian Institute and in Congress, and to really learn the workings of government. During these trips, I often visited the National Cathedral in Washington and heard Gregorian chant performed live by Benedictine monks. Their singing was of a very high quality. Later in my life, I heard Gregorian chant at the Vatican in Rome.

Are you interested in the physiological effects of chant and its tones?
Pelletier: Yes. There is good research on that, although not necessarily in reference to Gregorian chant. The brain and central nervous system is a finely tuned electrical and bio-electro magnetic system that consists of very subtle frequencies. These frequencies can be influenced by thought, they can be influenced by light, and they can be influenced by sound. Our ordinary active mode of processing information is characterized by what's known as beta electrical activity. It's a very fast frequency, quite random, and not very synchronous. If you could just look purely at the beta activity of the

brain, you would see something rather disorganized and asymmetrical, with some parts of the brain appearing extremely active while others appeared relatively inactive. If you dropped down one level lower to the next bandwidth, to an area that's become known, rather infamously, as the alpha state, you would see brain activity that appeared more uniform, more harmonic, and, if you just looked at the electrical tracings from the brain, it would appear more rhythmic, quieter, and relaxed. Now, in fact, you can induce more alpha activity in people by having them listen to classical music as opposed to rock music, to take two extremes. When a person listens to classical music, their brainwaves will literally slow down, and the brain become more synchronous. The feeling of subjective peacefulness that a person might report would be exactly what you would see in the brain itself. The subjective quality would, in turn, influence the brain. And there may also be some direct influence by certain sounds, through the auditory areas of the brain, by generating a sympathetic resonance that slows the brain down as a whole. So that's one of the ways that music is a direct mediator of deeper and more tranquil and peaceful states.

There are now some very practical applications of music in medicine, including its use before and during surgery and as a way to help people tolerate uncomfortable procedures, such as bronchoscopy.

In your writings, you are very interested in the importance of joy and the occasional exalted state.
Pelletier: I think there can be enormous benefits psychologically, physically, perhaps even spiritually, from such experiences. Before his death, Norman Cousins pointed out, rightfully, that while we know about the destructive effects of the negative emotions such as anger and depression—both of which predispose to major chronic diseases— we do not have a comparable body of knowledge about such positive emotions as altruism, love, inspiration, and compassion. He termed this area or research the "psychobiology of the positive emotions" and even funded projects, including several on humor. He was a friend for twenty years and influenced my thinking early on.

Protracted stress produces an increase in the stress hormones such as adrenaline and cortisd, which can be good, except when it goes on for too long a period of time and the catabolic processes, which generate energy for the body, begin actually to break down and burn up the body. But what you have with the positive emotions, as in meditation, or, I suspect, in someone enjoying music or singing, is that the anabolic processes, or biologically regenerative functions, predominate. You have lower metabolic rates, you have calcium being deposited in the bones, you have cellular regrowth. You literally have, during positive emotions, regeneration of your body.

So that's quite literally what's occurring at the physical level, but let's look for a moment at the psychological benefits of the joy of music. With so much more stress and demand on our lives, I think it's not coincidental that people are looking toward a more spiritual, more transcendent kind of experience, and finding that in some musics. It didn't surprise me that the recent album *Chant*, by the Benedictine monks of Santo Domingo de Silos, would be so moving to people, although reportedly it was a surprise to the marketing department.

We know that certain psychologically positive emotions, such as optimism and a sense of hardiness, can actually predict a person's likelihood of mental and physical health better than their physical, biological condition. Someone may have arthritis, as an example, and have a comparable level of joint deterioration to another person, but if the first individual is optimistic, has a sense of active coping, stays involved with people, in other words engages the positive end of the continuum, they will experience lower pain, have lower medication use and greater mobility, and have many fewer days of disability than the person who has the same level of potential biological disability but is less positive emotionally. So you can see that the positive emotions and conditions that elicit those emotions, such as music, can have a profound impact on health.

This reminds me of your famous phrase, "mind as healer, mind as slayer." Do you feel that through the judicious listening to certain enjoyable music we can help heal ourselves?
Pelletier: Absolutely. Every now and then, in the course of seeing patients, I have recommended music—in the same way that you would recommend a good book: "Have you read such and such? It relates to your situation." It could be chant, or contemporary music, or something from New Age artists, such as Kitaro or Stephen Halpern. Some of the New Age music is very inspirational and positive. Several years ago, a professor of psychology at UC Berkeley, Dr. William Soskin, who has since died, developed a method of therapeutic intervention around the deliberate use of specific tracks of classical music. It was meant to elicit emotional states that the person could then work on. But I've never become that sophisticated about it.

What do you think accounts for the tremendous popularity of chant music in the United States today?
Pelletier: I think we are at that point in time when we are asking questions about deeper meanings, values, and spirituality. And when we begin to ask such questions, then meditation, chant, and spiritually inspiring music become of greater rather than lesser interest. While too large a percentage of the population still lives below a desir-

able level of material wealth for our society, the majority of the people have adequate education, shelter, and clothing. When people reach a point of material satisfaction, they say to themselves, "Well, now what? What's next?" After the basic biological and safety needs are met, questions about the deeper meaning of existence occur to people, and occur *collectively* in cultures.

The post-war baby boomers, who are now the post-war gray boomers, seem to be the ones who are purchasing this kind of sacred music, and they clearly have the most discretionary income. These are the people who are looking for values beyond material satisfaction. They certainly are the people I see at conferences and rituals involving sacred music.

Do you still listen to chant?
Pelletier: Absolutely. There are two or three albums I listen to, the best known being *Chant*. And there is a brief piece sung by the Boy's Choir of Westminster Abbey that I really love. It's on the soundtrack of the film *Empire of the Sun*. Another recording I listen to is entitled *Rosa Mystica*, a quite remarkable piece of music produced by Therese Schroeder-Sheker, a musicologist. She was researching medieval music and discovered that there had once been a medieval monastic order in Cluny, France, that had a form of chanting that was directly related to physical and spiritual healing, and that also was specifically intended to ease the transition of people between life and death. The monks would minister to the dying and to the ill, and chant and play music at the point of the individual's death. It is not a well-known variant of chant, but it is a variant that is really very moving and powerful.

I tend to get up very early in the mornings—four or four-thirty is my time of day—and, as I drive to Stanford at that very early hour and observe the sun rising over San Francisco Bay, I'll often listen to the music we have been talking about. I find it just a great way to orient to the day.

Why have many of the world's religions brought chant to the bedside of the dying?
Pelletier: The point of chant and ritualistic music is to uplift and to remind us of the spiritual aspect of ourselves. At the time of death, the mind and spirit is often at its most subtle, and emotions such as fear reach their greatest height. One intention of chanting at this time is to allow the transition between life and death to occur with as much peace and equanimity as possible. A most notable example of this is the use by Tibetan monks of chant, music, and readings from the *Tibetan Book of the Dead* to guide the spirit in its transition between the material and nonmaterial reality.

If you are with a patient at the moment of death, you find that all the neurological and biological systems become slower and more subtle, if you will. By virtue of just that occurence, it is very likely, at a purely biological level, that music will have a much greater influence at the time of death than normally. It's perhaps similar to listening to music as you begin to fall asleep. At that time you find that you can pay closer attention to music; it has more of an emotional impact because you are more susceptible, more relaxed, more open.

> Chant is a form of spiritual tourism. It promises the contemporary soul a virtual reality, a virtual sanctity.
>
> **Katherine Bergeron**
> PROFESSOR OF MUSICOLOGY
> UNIVERSITY OF CALIFORNIA,
> BERKELEY

Are you familiar with types of chanting other than Gregorian chant?
Pelletier: The other form of chanting I'm most familiar with is that of the Gyuto Buddhist monks of Tibet. If you listen to the sound of their chanting, as opposed to trying to decipher their words (which I certainly can't), you realize that it sounds very similar to Gregorian chant. It has a very similar emotional impact on the listener. The Gyuto monks always state, very explicitly, that the sounds, in and of themselves, have a religious significance, and that they have the power to induce an uplifted or altered state.

A third tradition, which I have heard live, is the American Indian, in particular the Navaho or Dineh chants. They have three categories of chants—the *holy way*, *ghost way*, and *life way*. Within the *holy way* chants are the *blessing way* chants and rituals used for healing. Specific chants are used for specific illnesses, and learning a single chant can take years since they are as long as an epic poem. Today these chants are used by an entire community, in conjunction with conventional medicine, to help individuals.

If you listen to the Navaho chanting independently of the ability to understand the language, you notice some of the same overtones, some of the same inflections, as the other two traditions. There is the repetition in cycles of very specific patterns of sound. The element of duration is important—the chanting goes on for many, many minutes, sometimes hours, frequently accompanied by dance movement or rocking and swaying, which we know can also induce an altered state of consciousness. So you see that there are some parallels between these three forms of sacred chant. In fact, when the Dalai Lama visited the Southwest—I believe it was about three years ago—he and his entourage chanted with some of the Native American people, and he noted that there were very marked similarities between the ways that they both used chant to induce higher spiritual states of consciousness.

In all three traditions, then, chant is being used to raise consciousness and, broadly speaking, to heal?

Pelletier: Yes. They do state, quite explicitly, that the purpose of the chant is to heal the mind, heal the body, and elevate the spirit. The predominant purpose, I would say, is to elevate the spirit, and then, secondly, to heal the mind and body. That really is its intent—to align those three dimensions of ourselves and create a harmony. Increasingly, as we come to know that the human body is a very subtle bioelectromagnetic harmonic system, we are beginning to realize just how sensitive we are to sound, both sounds we utter and sounds that come from outside—more sensitive than we ever believed.

It is also interesting to consider the effects produced on people when they are chanting in a group, or when they are listening to a choir with others. You can literally feel a choir, or feel the monks, when they chant. The sound literally penetrates you, almost like a sonogram does. In the case of liturgy chanted in a cathedral, you have the effect of the acoustics. You get resonance, and overtones, and the bouncing around and amplification of sound. Cathedrals, such as England's Westminster Abbey, are designed to have very particular acoustics that pronounce the effect of the sound on those chanting and those who are listening. It is a deliberate attempt to induce a kind of otherworldliness to the sound.

Again, looking at chant neurologically, probably what happens when people are chanting together is that their central nervous system activity becomes synchronous; they become like, or of, one mind. Their stress hormones decrease, muscle tension decreases, and the heart rate normalizes. Those chanting would have a great deal more oxygen in their systems than normal, just by virtue of breathing in and out. You can think of it as a controlled hyperventilation, and we know that when people hyperventilate they enter into altered states. They feel high. They have a certain clarity of mind, and sometimes of physical vision. All of this would be enhanced by people chanting in groups.

That's a purely physical-level description. I also think that there is a psychologically uplifting effect from knowing that you and thirty people, or fifty people, or hundreds of people, have the same concerted, collective intent to celebrate something that is positive in life and in ourselves. That's very powerful, and I think all of us have been in groups and experienced it.

It's important to add that as much as I as a scientist, or anyone, can become enamored, so to speak, by the remarkable neurological and physiological phenomena of chanting, it would be an error in the extreme to reduce the power and the purpose and the effects of chanting to mere neurophysiology. It's ridiculous to be reductionist, to say "Look at this extraordinary spiritual event that has been occurring over hundreds of years, involving millions of people. Let's reduce it to some neurophysiology and biochemistry." That's not it at all. That reductionist view does a disservice to both science and spirituality. The significance resides in the chant itself and what it does for people.

Gregorian chant is termed sacred music. It carries the liturgy of the Roman Catholic Church. How might people who have not been brought up in that faith, or consider themselves not to have a faith, relate to Gregorian chant?

Pelletier: In the book *Sound Mind, Sound Body*, I had to differentiate between spiritual and religious. Religion is the spiritual experience interpreted by a particular orientation, be it Catholic, Jewish, Buddhist, or another religion. Spirituality is the event itself, the uplifting of consciousness, the higher order of experience, the ineffable—the kinds of things that poets, artists, and musicians convey more adequately than science ever has. And I would place chant in the category of a spiritual experience because it is independent of an understanding of the words. At one point in my life, I could understand the Latin, and although I don't anymore, it doesn't matter. I personally have had friends with me in the presence of chant—Tibetan, Catholic, and American Indian chant—and they were as moved as I was, having absolutely no understanding intellectually of what it meant.

So chant is transcendent. It's not owned. In the case of Gregorian chant, it may be a Catholic liturgical practice, formalized by Pope Gregory I about 600 AD, but its influence is infinitely greater than that. It has an ability to convey to people an experience of a higher order spirituality.

> Gregorian chant was sung daily when I was being trained in the seminary to be a priest. For centuries it had been the main way of praying to God in the monasteries and seminaries of the Catholic Church. The simplicity of the melodies had an effect on the souls of those singing them. One was not distracted by unusual melodies. One concentrated more on what the psalm was saying to God. As a result, it was a powerful way of trying to make contact with God in prayer.
>
> **Fr. Malcolm O'Leary**
>
> ROMAN CATHOLIC PRIEST
> HOLY GHOST PARISH,
> OPELOUSAS, LOUISIANA

3

Rediscovering Gregorian Chant in the New Millennium

Chant for the Masses

by Richard Crocker

N 1994 AN event occurred unprecedented in the thousand-year history of Gregorian chant. A compact disc recording of chant, sung by monks in a monastery, sold a very large number of copies, mostly to listeners who had little or no experience with chant, or with monasteries. (The CD, by the Benedictine Monks of the Abbey of Santo Domingo de Silos, was released by Angel Records under the title *Chant*. Angel CD 55138.)

There was, in fact, nothing unusual about the recording itself. The monks of Silos had made previous recordings, released during the preceding decade, but only people with special interest noticed them. The real event in 1994 was the enormous popularity. That the music was beautiful, and meaningful to a great many people, was inescapably obvious. But why was it suddenly so popular? Thoughtful listeners, noting the extreme distance between the ninth-century monastic context of Gregorian chant and twentieth-century urban life, wondered about the propriety of our response. Were we responding to the chant as it really was, or was the mass popularity a function of a whimsical, ephemeral taste for the novel and unusual— or worse still, the result of media hype? Or was the popular reaction something more, a response to aspects of the chant that are independent of social context, and even of *intended* meaning?

These are questions that concern our appreciation of a great deal of music from long ago and far away. Gregorian chant seems *so* remote, however, and the popularity of *Chant* was so great so suddenly, that it has thrust these questions up front. It has been suggested that the marketing and pro-

motional procedures had their cynical aspects, and it *is* observable that the various pro-
motional materials were as expedient and unreliable as advertising can be expected to
be. Careful analysis may have more to say on the subject; perhaps we will not want to
hear it. In any case, it would not change the basic fact that a great many people have
responded strongly to Gregorian chant. In other words, the marketing brought the
chant to the attention of the mass audience, who at that point were ready to receive it.
So the crucial aspects of the response have to do with that readiness—the context in
which the chant was received—rather than the context from which it came.

CRITICAL RESPONSES TO CHANT

EARLIER RECORDINGS OF GREGORIAN CHANT

Gregorian chant seems novel or unusual only to the mass audience. The first response
to the CD was from those of us—and there were very many—who had heard, admired,
and performed Gregorian chant for decades. Throughout this century Europeans and
Americans have actively cultivated Gregorian chant; we can say that there are chant traditions specific to our own time. These traditions have flourished in cathedrals and
parishes, as well as in monasteries and convents. Dom André Mocquereau
(1849–1930), one of the principals of the revival of Gregorian chant begun at the
Benedictine monastery of Solesmes (north of Paris), seems to have rejoiced more than
anything in a very well-trained parish choir, preferably of children, singing chant in the
style he imagined.

Dom Mocquereau emerged as guru to the many thousands of Roman
Catholics who have sung chant in our time. The genius of his method was its
near-universal comprehensibility—in practice even if not in its theory. I have had
the experience of singing chant with a complete stranger, as if from the other end
of the world, and enjoying on the first try perfect ensemble as well as authentic
Solesmes style.

There were other gurus with other methods, some of them as highly regarded as
his. To list them would be to index the most successful chant recordings of mid-centu-
ry. For there *were* numerous recordings long before 1994. They were issued on "78s,"
then on LPs, and some are now being reissued on CDs. I find that the old recordings
from Solesmes show a musical technique not surpassed by the newer recordings (I
speak of technique, not interpretation). The monks of Silos would be the first to
acknowledge the Solesmes technique; that is where they learned theirs.

> Listening to Gregorian chant has always had a remarkable effect on me, immediately turning down my usually high, rather frenetic, energy, while turning on a level of deeper inner calm. As the chants take me deeper into myself and out of myself, I feel a renewed bond with the Human Connection, as well as with my own sense of spirituality.
>
> **Philip Zimbardo,**
> PROFESSOR OF PSYCHOLOGY
> STANFORD UNIVERSITY

OBJECTIONS REGARDING AUTHENTICITY

A second response follows closely upon the first. It comes from chant scholars, few in number at first, but hard at work throughout the century, amassing much data and at least some insight. (The results are best and most easily seen in David Hiley's *Western Plainsong* [1993]; his listing of studies by previous scholars fills 64 pages.) Throughout the century these scholars have intensively debated various proposals for the authentic or appropriate way of singing the chant. Some scholars lay on the new recordings the same criticism they laid on Dom Mocquereau: "That is not how it sounded back then!" This initiates what to some of us is a fascinating, and usually heated, discussion. "How do we know how it sounded back then?" This in turn leads back to the question posed so forcefully by the popularity of the disc: "Does it make a difference how it sounded back then?"

One of the most interesting answers has been provided more recently by Dom Eugene Cardine, another monk at Solesmes, and a successor to Dom Mocquereau. Dom Cardine emphasized the importance of the performance directions included in some of the earliest chant books with musical notation (circa 900 AD). A group of Austrian and Italian scholars is actively pursuing Dom Cardine's lead, generating scholarly studies, and also chant recordings. Dom Cardine did not think much of Dom Mocquereau's method of performance, but did not seem to have one of his own. I find that these Austrian and Italian recordings do not yet fulfill the potential of Dom Cardine's approach. I believe that full and imaginative use of the early notation can lead to a new alternative perception and appreciation of Gregorian chant for the contemporary listener.

GREGORIAN CHANT AND MONASTICISM

A third response is an objection, sometimes delivered in a tone of righteous indignation: "Gregorian chant is monastic. Therefore you have to be monastic in order to understand it. Most modern listeners are not monastic, therefore most do not understand the chant, and the popularity of the recording is based on a complete misunderstanding by the mass audience." This objection implies some of the basic questions underlying the contemporary critical discussion about our response to chant: *How does music communicate meaning? Can a listener appreciate music without perceiving the composer's meaning? Is it necessary to know the intended meaning in the original context in order to hear it in the music?"*

People who write about music go round and round with such questions, often without even asking them. In the present case, one point of view asserts that non-monastics simply cannot appreciate Gregorian chant; or, if we try, we will miss some important part of the meaning; or, if we want to learn to appreciate it, we must find out all we can about monasticism and listen to the chant as if we were monastic. But while many people in the mass audience may be fascinated by, or at least curious about monasticism, it is clear that the mass audience listened to and enjoyed the disc without benefit of knowing a great deal about monasticism. Therefore (it is asserted) they were responding to something other than the true meaning of the chant. This may trouble a thoughtful listener.

To judge the validity of the objection we need better factual information about monasticism and monastic music than I have so far brought to bear. Therefore, I will review a few relevant facts and insights that chant scholarship has produced.

WHICH CHANT IS AUTHENTIC GREGORIAN CHANT?

What is commonly called "Gregorian chant" includes several repertories of sacred song accumulated over more than a thousand years. While some chants from the thirteenth century, or the seventeenth, or the twentieth, may be the same kind of music as the earliest chant from the eighth century, many other chants from the later centuries are very different. Furthermore, the term "Gregorian chant" is sometimes used not with reference to musical style but instead to other aspects having to do with the kind of words being sung, or with the kind of voices that are singing, or the kind of occasion for which they are singing. For instance, a male chorus singing the traditional Latin words for the Roman Catholic Mass has, on occasion, been said to be singing "Gregorian chant." In order to refer more precisely to a specific historical repertory, however, many scholars apply "Gregorian" only to the repertory developed in the seventh and eighth centuries and written down in the ninth and tenth centuries. As it happens, the nineteen selections on *Chant* are drawn mostly from repertory documented as coming from the tenth century, and therefore are "Gregorian" in this strictly delimited scholarly sense (at least four items, however, are post-Gregorian).

That much is merely a matter of labeling, but if we go on to say "Gregorian chant is *only monastic* chant" we are making a substantive assertion—and one that is not the case. Most of *Chant* is *not* monastic chant; at least, not in any sense that would require its meaning to be understood only in a monastic context. Only four items ("Mandatum novum," "Media vita," "Verbum caro," "Genuit puerpera") can be called monastic, and they are not distinctively so. This statement requires some explanation.

MONASTERY AND CATHEDRAL CHANT

Liturgists have for some time distinguished between cathedral liturgies and monastic liturgies. These represent very different contexts. Cathedral worship is public, primarily for ordinary Christian men, women, and children in the secular world, usually urban; it also is designed to attract and impress a wider public, unconverted but interested. Monastic worship, on the other hand, is reserved for the dedicated monastic community. It forms part of their unceasing vigil of meditation and praise. Gregorian chant (in the restricted sense of the early repertory) has a corresponding division into chant developed for cathedral purposes, and chant developed for special, distinctively monastic purposes. The liturgy of the Mass and the Eucharist (the primary Christian celebration, with communion of bread and wine) was in place by the end of the first century AD; its locale was the cathedral. Protoforms of morning and evening prayer emerged in the second and third centuries, also in the context of the cathedral. Only after that did Christian monasticism appear, its special liturgies defined in the fourth, fifth, and sixth centuries. Even though Gregorian chant as we know it from the early repertory did not take shape until the seventh or eighth century, when it did it was fashioned in accord with the purposes appropriate to its liturgies: Chant for Mass was for public ceremonial, as was chant for morning and evening prayer; for the monastic night-and-day perpetual cycle of meditation, other kinds of chant were developed, and they were different from the Mass chants. (Mass, of course, was sung in monasteries—eventually even more frequently than in cathedrals—but for this the monasteries used the forms of worship and music developed in the cathedrals.)

Most of the chant on the disc is cathedral chant. When we listen to it, we can with complete propriety imagine the context of a downtown cathedral. Perhaps we came in as curious pagans, and were overwhelmed by the sights of ritual pageantry, the smells of incense, and the sheer musical beauty of the chant.

WHAT WOULD BE "MONASTIC CHANT"?

Distinctively monastic liturgies are in the perpetual night-and-day cycle of praise and meditation called the "Divine Office." While the main parts of the day-time cycle—morning prayer ("Lauds") and evening prayer ("Vespers")—came from cathedral liturgy, the night-time cycle of "Nocturns" is monastic. The singing of the Nocturns, sometime between midnight and dawn, corresponds best to the popular image of monasticism evoked by the *Chant* disc. The Nocturns, sung every night, are long and complex; they involve singing a great deal of material from the Bible and other religious literature. Taking account of the musical elements, there are four principal types of characteristically monastic Nocturn chant:

Psalmody: the singing of complete Psalms in a numerical order,
using *psalm tones* (short formulas repeated for every verse).
The father of Western monasticism, St. Benedict, who codified a
basic form of monasticism in his *Rule* circa 530, required a
minimum of twelve Psalms each night.

Lection tones: for the readings from the Bible (up to twelve during
the night); each lesson is read mostly on one pitch, with simple
formulas of three or four other pitches for punctuation.

Antiphons: short melodies sung in various kinds of alternation
with Psalms and other items.

Responsories: longer, much more elaborate melodies; one is sung
after each lesson.

These are substantial repertories; medieval manuscripts may supply up to 2,000 antiphons, and over 1,000 responsories. Except for stray borrowings and adaptations, these melodies are not sung at Mass.

Psalmody is the most distinctive form of monastic chant, the form most remote from ordinary notions of music; many people, when they refer to "chant" or "chanting," have psalmody in mind. If someone who had in mind only this monotonic chanting encountered for the first time the rich melodies of, say, the "Gradual Chants" on the disc ("Os iusti," "Christus factus est," "Laetatus sum," "Iacta cogitatum," "Oculi omnium"), they might well be amazed that such music could come from such a remote context. Perhaps this is one reason the music on the disc seemed so novel, and so interesting. There are, however, only two short Psalms on the disc (Psalms 99, 132). These two Psalms each have an antiphon, and since the Psalms themselves are so short, their antiphons are the more prominent element. While antiphons are widely used in monastic music, their use is optional; and they are not so distinctively monastic, being also used in cathedral chant. There are two responsories on the disc ("Media vita," "Verbum caro"); the first of these is performed with much repetition, which is characteristic of monastic chant in the Nocturns. Like antiphons, responsories are similar to some cathedral music, and not so distinctively monastic.

On other recordings of recent decades there has been much more monastic chant, and occasionally a truly representative portion of a Nocturn. Nocturns can give a sense of timelessness and inner repose because of the long stretches of monotonic repetitive musical patterns. But such recordings have not appealed to the mass audience. The appeal of *Chant* is due to its cathedral chant, not its monastic chant, but I am not suggesting that the monks of Silos avoided monastic chant for the sake of greater appeal.

The cathedral chant on the disc has been selected from a repertory that carefully assigns each of about 500 items of chant to a specific function at Mass on a specific calendar day. The liturgical context of a given chant includes (1) the other chants assigned to be sung before and after it, (2) the ritual activity going on around and during the singing of the chant, (3) the meaning of the words in terms of the theme of that particular occasion, whether feast day (such as Christmas) or a saint's day. On the disc the chant is not presented in any context that can be called liturgical (and since in this recording, as in so many others, we cannot make out what words they are singing, we get no help there either). The cathedral chant has been ripped from its liturgical context, and presented as an object of purely musical contemplation. *This is a peculiarly monastic mode of using music.* It involves meditation on a mantra-like object as a path to

> The effect of Gregorian chant is not a matter of being transported, or of sort of losing touch with reality because of the power of the music. Nevertheless, the singing of these texts does lift one out of the plane of ordinary speech. And that is doubtless an important part of their creating a kind of atmosphere, or context, for what is in the end worship.
>
> **Don Randel**
> PROFESSOR OF MUSICOLOGY AND PROVOST, CORNELL UNIVERSITY

> When I was teaching third grade for the Orange County Unified School District, my students liked listening to Gregorian chant. They related to the male vocals and the repetition because they found it familiar. They also preferred it to rap music. We would compare and contrast rap with chant and, although they liked both, they chose to listen to Gregorian chant because it was more relaxing and less distracting.
>
> **Kelly Ruggirello**
> DIRECTOR OF EDUCATION
> AND COMMUNITY PROGRAMS
> THE PACIFIC SYMPHONY ORCHESTRA

mystic ascent. Paradoxically, this recording encourages a listener to hear the music as a powerful stimulus to inner experience—with no reference to liturgy or religion or monasticism beyond what the listener chooses to bring. "Monastic," then, can have more than one meaning.

The Benedictines have always placed even elaborate chant at the center of monastic life, and this shows simply how irrelevant to an understanding of Gregorian chant is the question whether it is monastic. Monasteries use the chant, or not, for their own purposes; they can do that—and so can we.

IS GREGORIAN CHANT RELIGIOUS MUSIC?
Early in the twentieth century, the Benedictines of Solesmes, by much urging, got the Vatican to issue confirmation that Gregorian chant should be some kind of standard for Roman Catholic music. But the Second Vatican Council (1964), reflecting popular pressure, allowed Gregorian chant, along with Latin and the traditional forms of the Mass, to slip into more or less honorable retirement. The Benedictines of Solesmes may have hoped in the first half of the century that their chant book, the *Liber usualis*, would become the musical Bible of every parish; and it did become widely used. But with Vatican II the *Liber usualis* has gone out of print, and the Benedictines have been scrambling to find some viable use for their Gregorian material.

The disc presents Gregorian chant in the sounds most likely to be acceptable as music for Catholic worship. One result is that a great many people—non-Catholics included—seem willing to grant that this music is not inappropriate to religious worship. They correctly identify the rich echoey sound, the smooth melodic flow with no articulation, and the slow, undifferentiated tempo as compatible with twentieth century Euro-American conservative well-bred religiosity. I doubt very much, however, that is why they went out to buy the disc.

WHY DID IT SELL?

Why did it sell and why would we want to know that? Recording companies, obviously, want to know what sells. More generally, musicians want to know what appeals. In arts of all kinds this is a perennial question. Because it concerns art, there is no scientific answer: Artists go with hunches, inner conviction, and they know what succeeds only when it succeeds. Similarly with marketers. People interested in the monastic life may want to see in the popularity of *Chant* a renewed interest in monasticism. My own interest as a historian is in finding a way to understand this popularity within the framework of European musical history as I have constructed it in my mind.

THE TEXTURE OF CHANT

The chant on the disc, like all Gregorian chant (in the strictly historical sense), comes to us one note at a time; its texture is "monophonic." Compared to more familiar music, there is no accompaniment, no chordal harmony, no counterpoint, and no use of instruments. It is a kind of music one person can sing alone—it requires only one voice sounding. The fact that more than one voice is singing (but still on one note at a time) is an important aspect of the *timbre*.

So the texture of this chant is different from almost all the other music in classical as well as popular repertories. And yet it does not sound *completely* different. One listener may find the simple texture deficient, but another listener may hardly notice the absence, until it is pointed out. And in other aspects, the chant sounds to some listeners the same as classical or popular music. Classical or popular may not be heard by many people as harmony or counterpoint at all. (Another possibility is that harmony and counterpoint may not be so basic to the musical experience as music theorists sometimes make out.) In any case, the texture of chant is made different by leaving out sounds that we might expect; and it does not replace the missing sounds with other unexpected or alien sounds. In this respect, chant leaves the listener room: The ears are not filled with a welter of sound demanding to be heard in a certain way.

"AS IF WITH ONE VOICE"

The chant on the disc is sung by a male chorus, with a timbre or tone quality that is very familiar to contemporary listeners. If it is different, it is different in the same way that the texture is different: Nothing accompanies the male chorus, there is no other timbre supporting or competing, as there would be even in a chorus that included female voices. There are no instruments that, if added even without changing the texture (that is, playing exactly what the voice sang), would also change the timbre, per-

haps drastically. Absent from the disc is the timbre of a solo voice. Such timbres have much more individual character than does a chorus; one need only imagine the effect of Placido Domingo's voice, or Bruce Springsteen's, to understand how well-defined is the timbre of the male chorus, even while it is unassuming. (There are medieval legends that tell of the consequences attendant upon a mysterious stranger with a strong, very beautiful voice entering the chapel and singing along with the monks in the Nocturns.) Other factors that affect the quality of sound on the disc are that the singing is generally in tune--not perfectly, but very good; also that the voices are matched and blend well; and that the vocal sound is not pushed, but rather floats easily. Altogether this makes for easy listening. It is also anonymous: No individual voice speaks. It is more like a large cello section of a good orchestra.

In the beginning, and still today in some circumstances, Gregorian chant included sections for solo voice, and sometimes these sections made a brilliant contrast to the chorus sections. Early on there seems to have been objection to such contrast, or at any rate a preference for using the less individual sound of two, three, or four singers performing as a sub-set (identified as "cantors") instead of a solo singer. This happens on the *Chant* disc: The sections sung by the cantors are not obvious, but when they are located, they will be heard to reveal slightly more individual timbres, slightly less blend than the chorus. The preference for this practice may be traced back to the great popularity among early Christians of a hymn in the Book of Daniel (3, 51-90), in which the three young men cast into the fiery furnace praise God "as if with one voice."

ACOUSTIC CONTEXT
All the chant on the disc is performed in a very resonant, echoey space, and this is a very important aspect of the timbre. It makes it sound "churchy," an *association* placed upon the quality of the sound. Nonetheless, increase of resonance is a perfectly common practice of enhancement, widely used and valued in many different kinds of music today. It complements the male-chorus timbre in creating a sound that is smooth yet rich, full of potential meaning that is not clearly articulated.

The acoustic resonance also creates a sense of distance. This can be accentuated by listening to the disc from the next room, where it may sound even better. This raises the question of who is listening to a performance that gets better the further away and less distinct it is. It must be someone standing at the back of the church, observing but not engaged in the performance. The sound is different if heard by someone standing close to the singers, or by the singers themselves. Would the music then mean something different?

Pitch that is intoned clearly, one pitch at a time, especially with resonance and distance, can have a magical effect--and apparently has always had this effect. Intonation can be close to incantation. For this to happen, pitches need to be perceived separately and clearly, as they can be perceived on *Chant*, and in chant generally. In turn, the effects of intonation can greatly enhance the musical experience of chant. I believe that this magical effect compensates for the lack of harmony, counterpoint, instrumental accompaniment, and other features of contemporary music.

CAN WE UNDERSTAND MUSIC THAT IS NOT IN THE MODERN TONAL SYSTEM?

Observers often say that the pitch configuration of Gregorian chant is sufficiently different from Euro-American music to not be meaningful in terms of modern pitch configurations, or to be meaningful only in some very different way, perhaps meaningful only as expression of the monastic life, or of mysticism. Observers might go on to say that with no harmony and no tonality, Gregorian chant must have a different tonal structure, and use a different type of melody. It is this point of view (if it acknowledges that the mass audience finds true meaning in the chant) that looks to context to explain the popularity of the disc; for this point of view asks, How could the mass audience understand the music simply from its sound?

Recourse is usually had to "modes" and "modality" to explain Gregorian tonal structure. But most specialists now agree that the Gregorian repertory in the strict sense came into being prior to and independently of the system of modes we find documented; and the system we find later in the Middle Ages neither conflicts with nor adds much to the tonal system in use throughout European music. This is the *diatonic* system, conveniently at hand in the white keys of the piano. (Think of it not so much as a scale—especially not as a C-major scale—but rather as a set of pitches displayed in a row.) This is the basic pitch set in use from Gregorian chant until now. Listeners know their way around it through sheer familiarity. There is no problem in hearing Gregorian chant moving within this pitch set; the only problem for the modern listener is to refrain from importing a more specific system that attempts to interpret the diatonic. The specific system most apt to be imported is the one that we use to interpret classical and popular music. This system hears the diatonic in terms of a specific scale that has a beginning, note number 1 (the "tonic"), which is heard as a reference point for the other notes. The tonic is heard also as a center of gravity, of repose--a place to end. All of that works well for classical and popular music, less well for Gregorian chant and other early music that was developed before the tonic system came into use. For

hearing Gregorian chant, we *must* hear the diatonic system (whose use goes back far before Gregorian), and *need not* import the tonic system. This the mass audience can do easily, and I believe has done. *Consciously or unconsciously, they seem to have understood the chant in the appropriate tonal system, and this understanding provides a base for the popularity of the disc.*

THE MYSTERY OF GREGORIAN MELODY

The tonal system, then, seems to me to be the least problematic aspect of hearing Gregorian chant; I find more problems in the melodic detail—the particular ways in which the melody moves through the diatonic system. These ways are idiosyncratic and peculiar to the repertory. The fact that they are different from classical and popular music contributes to the sense of remoteness of Gregorian chant, possibly to a sense of mysticism. While use of the diatonic makes for easy, almost automatic listening, the melodic idiom suggests some musical sense that is hidden, unfamiliar, and only dimly perceptible.

Can this melodic idiom become familiar? Can it be learned? In part, certainly, and easily; but for me the most fascinating feature of Gregorian chant is that, after forty years of close familiarity, this idiom seems to me in some respects no more familiar than when I first heard it. There seems to be something about the pitch configurations of Gregorian chant that resists systematic tracking; it does not readily reveal its nature. That in itself is a basic kind of meaning, involving mystery; this is a kind of mystery that is in the music, not in the context. And it in no way inhibits a strong response to the chant.

In shaping phrases, Dom Mocquereau worked primarily with rhythm, but this turned out to be a matter of shaping the pitch configurations. And while he did not import the tonic system into chant, Dom Mocquereau did import, or construct, phrase shapes that can feel familiar to us, and this is one reason scholars have been critical of his interpretation. When these phrase shapes are made too explicit in performance, the result sounds overdone. For instance, the slowing down at the ends of phrases is sometimes extreme, and an expressive note may be lingered over too lovingly. I believe this kind of performance is an important factor in the popularity of the disc, as well as an important factor in the *reservations* about the disc held by many of those who had worked with chant long before the disc appeared.

WILL GREGORIAN CHANT REMAIN POPULAR?

At the same time that I find Gregorian melody to be hidden in certain respects, I believe its pitch configurations are very, very good--so good that they can speak, or better, sing to us directly, no matter how they are performed, no matter what the context or the interpretation. And the melodies sing of something that is different from classical and popular music. *Chant* made the valuable demonstration that Gregorian chant could be made popular, and *not* through a deliberate manipulation of musical resources or because of a mere chance coincidence of factors.

In the wake of that success, music marketers are trying their luck; but that is a matter of business, without musical significance. What is of great potential significance is that musicians may use this opportunity to make Gregorian chant a more integral part of our contemporary experience of performing and listening. As that happens, the chant will be sung in ways more clearly articulated, and more individual. But then different renditions of the chant, each speaking more strongly, will speak only to smaller segments of the mass audience; by intent and necessity, they will not repeat the one-time phenomenon of the disc. ■

A Listening Guide

❦

TO AN ELEVENTH-CENTURY MARIAN ANTIPHON:
"ALMA REDEMPTORIS MATER"
(LOVING MOTHER OF THE REDEEMER)

by Robert Winter

Perhaps the most beautiful of the Marian antiphons is *Alma redemptoris mater* (Loving Mother of the Redeemer), one of the few early plainchants to be ascribed to a particular author. It is thought to have been written by Hermann of Reichenau (1013?–1054), better known as Hermannus Contractus (Herman the Cripple), although certain stylistic features of the piece suggest a date of about a century later.

The melody of *Alma redemptoris mater* is treated very differently from what we would expect in a traditional tonal melody. Except for one brief rise outside the mode, the melody remains within the octave above the final. This plainchant consists of four sections. The first section rises from the final to f an octave above and then descends again. The other three sections consist of highly embellished descents from f. Section Two descends only to a, but Sections Three and Four descend to the final.

We find in this music examples of the three types of text setting that were common in early plainchant. The first section opens with an elaborate *melisma*, in which a single syllable (*Al-*(ma), a reference to Mary's loving nature) is sung to more than five or six notes (our *melisma* contains fourteen notes). At the other end of the spectrum we find *syllabic* writing, in which each syllable receives only a single note. Between these two extremes is *neumatic* writing, in which a syllable receives several notes. These categories represent points on a continuum, and the music moves freely from one style to the other.

A practice common to many plainchants was the use of melodic patterns, or formulas, that are repeated in the course of the melody. An example is the third phrase of

Section One (*quae pervia caeli*), whose nine notes differ only slightly from the eight notes of the second phrase in Section Four (*ac posterius*).

Such repetitions lend the plainchant a sense of serenity and balance.

Plainchant was notated with *neumes* rather than with note values and barlines. Consequently, most modern transcriptions use noteheads with neither stems nor barlines, making it easier to follow the gentle rise and fall of the lines.

LISTENING GUIDE

Although it flows smoothly from beginning to end in a predominantly neumatic style, *"Alma redemptoris mater"* divides into four sections, the last three of which contain varied descents from the highest note. The most extended melisma occurs on "Al-(ma)" at the very opening, underscoring Mary's loving nature.

Text	Comments
Section 1	
Alma redemptoris mater,	Long melisima on first syllable. Climbs
Loving mother of the Redeemer,	from final to highest note, and back.
quae pervia caeli porta manes,	Melisima on *"porta manes"*
who art the open door into heaven	
Section 2	
et stella maris, succurre cadenti	Descends from the highest note to
and star of the sea, aid thy people,	
a surgere qui curat populo;	
who fall but strive to stand again;	
Section 3	
Tu quae genuisti,	Descends from the
Thou who gave birth	highest note to the final.
natura mirante,	Neumatic setting
to nature's amazement,	
tuum sanctorium genitorem;	
to the holy Creator;	
Section 4	
Virgo prius ac posterius,	Descends, largely in a neumatic setting,
yet ceased not to be a virgin,	from the highest note to the final.
Gabrielis ab ore	
receiving from Gabriel's lips	
sumens illud Ave peccatorum miserere	*Miserere* is set syllabically.
that greeting *Ave*, havemercy on us sinners.	

A Female Voice in the Choir

by Ismael Fernandez de la Cuesta

"Let your women keep silence in the churches..." (1 Corinthians: 14,34). For centuries, within all-male communities, such as those of clergymen and monks, this mandate of Saint Paul was followed to the letter. So, in order to be able to perform polyphonic music with "mixed" voices, the choirs of the great churches, cathedrals, and monasteries maintained their own singing schools for boys, who were known as the *Pueri cantores*. (Wonderful examples of choruses of boys still remain; for example, the Vienna Boys' Choir and the Boys' Choir School of the Benedictine monastery of Montserrat in Spain.)

Often, just a few meters away from the monasteries that housed men, a monastery, or convent, for women would be built. Clearly, for their celebrations of the Mass, the nuns used to sing the same chants as the monks. A monastic rule called the *Regula communis*, written in Spain shortly after the year 656, called for mixed monasteries. These religious houses contained both monks and nuns, who resided in adjacent buildings. The men and women attended the same church and celebrated the liturgy together. Saint Benedict founded a nunnery in Montecassino, alongside the building where the monks lived. According to the biography written by Saint Gregory the Great, Saint Benedict buried his sister, Saint Scholastica, at the summit of Montecassino (*Dialogues*, book 2, chapter 33).

The discant "*Catholicorum concio*" was recovered from a thirteenth-century codex produced at the women's monastery at Las Huelgas in Burgos. Around the time this discant was composed and copied into manuscript form at Las Huelgas, there were several nuns renowned for their singing voices: Sancha Garcia (1204), Maria Garcia (1240), Maria Arias (1247), Ines-Agnes Gonzalez (1262), Maria Guillen y Urraca Garcia (1296), and Juana Sanchez de Porella (1343). These nuns definitely performed the chants that appear in the codex written at their monastery. It is very likely that the nuns even performed some of the pieces along with the Royal Choir whenever the King and Queen of Castile—whose court was located next to the monastery—attended the nuns' liturgical services.

Therefore, by introducing a female voice among the deep masculine voices of the Gregorian chant and its discants, I am attempting to re-create the sonorous world that existed within the church of the Monastery of Las Huelgas in Burgos during the thirteenth and fourteenth centuries. ■

Gregorian Chant Today

by Ismael Fernandez de la Cuesta

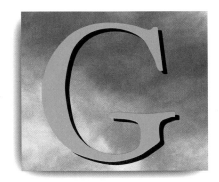

REGORIAN CHANT IS ancient, but not antiquated. It did not die and become forgotten until revived by modern musicologists. Although it has undergone infinite changes, it has remained alive through many centuries, and is still very much alive today.

Since the nineteenth century and up to the threshold of the twenty-first century, countless studies have been done on this traditional chant, but not one of these has been able to establish a unique or definitive mode for its singing, precisely because no such mode *ever* existed—neither at Gregorian chant's beginning nor during the course of its secular history.

The earliest liturgical music (transmitted by oral tradition) began to be preserved in written form in certain ninth-century codices that survive today. From the ninth century on, the technique of musical notation has allowed us to discover the two seemingly paradoxical qualities that give this chant its vitality: radical uniformity and outward unevenness. Both of these features are the result of innumerable mutations and accidents, as well as deliberate modifications, that occurred throughout the centuries in the many and diverse regions of the Western world.

The earliest codices of the ancient repertory utilize a very precise written code, known as *neumatic notation*. However, this ancient system only expresses the articulation of the continuous vocal sound. It does not adequately communicate two important elements of music— the duration (absolute and relative) of each sound and each sound's melodic position. Therefore, a chant cannot be performed solely with the aid of neumatic notation. A singer of Gregorian chant would also have to be familiar with the piece and rely upon his memory in order to perform it when using an early manuscript.

Over time, this primitive written code began to be improved upon and perfected. By the eleventh century, musical notation had become a means of conveying with great precision the rhythm and melody of a chant. Unfortunately, the more sophisticated technique of notation that replaced the neumatic system did not preserve many subtle, yet important, musical elements reflected in the original manuscripts.

Restoration of Gregorian chant in the nineteenth century was undertaken with the idea of rediscovering a version more representative of the actual music preserved in the most ancient codices. However, the information provided by the earliest manuscripts is far from complete. Neither the melody nor the exact rhythm of the chants is revealed. To complicate matters further, the later manuscripts offer some versions of the chant that seem decadent. For instance, the newer examples frequently assign a precise measured rhythm to each piece. Yet the very information we must infer about the character of the chant often contradicts the specific instructions previously set forth in neumatic notation.

During the twentieth century, a certain way of performing Gregorian chant spread throughout the world: performance according to the tradition of the School of the Abbey of Solesmes in France. The Solesmes monks arrived at a compromise between the interpretation of the data handed down by oral tradition and that derived from the oldest manuscripts. The most authentic chant was the monodic one: sounds produced by combining the ancient neumes with a musical rhythm, articulated in binary and ternary tempos. This technique produced an effect similar to the rhythm of intoned speech. At the same time, the voice was supposed to be used in a natural way, without special inflections. The message of the liturgical text sung in Latin was supposed to be *expressed* with the music itself.

> Gregorian chant is very concentrated music and, consequently, very dramatic. In retrospect, looking back over many years of listening to chant, it seems to me there is a correlation between it and the minimalist music of our own day, where the emphasis is on simplification rather than ornateness.
>
> **Ray Reinhardt**
> STAGE, FILM, AND TELEVISION ACTOR

This technique of chanting spread throughout the entire world and produced a break with the immediate *and* the remote past. A true cultural modification occurred. Gregorian chant had once more demonstrated itself to be a living art form.

In order to interpret Gregorian chant within the context considered decadent (when tropes and discant were introduced into the chant), the singer has various options. One of them is to assume the twentieth-century tradition, and the other is to try to perform the chant using the information provided by the written sources of earlier centuries.

From an artistic standpoint, the first option has been more than adequately explored. With respect to the second option, it is impossible to clear up all the doubts created by the codices themselves. We really do not know how the voice was used when these pieces were originally performed.

In the manuscripts of the thirteenth and fourteenth centuries, discants sometimes appear with a fixed rhythmic structure already indicated, to be sung with a measured tempo and *plausus*. Contemporary theorists have debated the manner in which these measured chants should be written and sung. What is certain is that when there was more than one discant voice, a measured rhythmic tempo was necessary to facilitate simultaneous consonance and harmony within the chant. If we wanted to sing the pieces obeying the manuscripts as well as modern theorists, we would be compelled for the sake of historical accuracy to perform the pieces with a measured beat. But this rule should not be applied *only* to the parts of the works endowed with discants, but also to the purely monodic parts. Therefore, Gregorian chant must have been sung note by note, attacking the sounds individually, without any other rhythmic articulation that could be produced by a continuous series of sounds modulated by words.

Today we are accustomed to hearing Gregorian chants sung by the finest choirs of our time. If the interpretation of the chant does not conform to the mensural rules proposed for discant by the theorists of the thirteenth and fourteenth centuries, the discant should then conform to the rhythms dictated by the usual Gregorian chant style. There could not have been a contradiction between the way one part and another of the same piece was performed.

Since the practice of discant preceded by many centuries the musician's ability to write polyphonic music with musical notations, it is obvious that, in an age when mensuralism was not yet developed, the discant was performed according to the rhythmic articulation of the principal voice. Thus, many of the pieces that appear in the manuscripts are not attributable to the period in which they were written, but to a more ancient time in which the melody was developed with freedom and not subjected to the rigidity of an artificial rhythmic superstructure.

The complexity of Gregorian chant's evolution has inevitably led to a great diversity in the interpretation of the music. Every choir has performed it in its own way. In the eighteenth century, for example, Jeronimo Romero, choir master of Toledo Cathedral, made his own arrangement of the chant for the members of his choir to perform. In contrast, during the nineteenth century, the monks of Solesmes insisted on basing their version of the chants on the oldest extant manuscripts. Also from Solesmes came Dom Eugenio Cardine's interesting musical semiology, carried out to give clearer guidelines for the interpretation of Gregorian chant. Far from insisting on the purely historical approach to the interpretation of Gregorian chant encouraged by Dom Gueranger (founder of the Abbey of Solesmes), today's musicologists take a more practical stance; they are prepared to search for the authentic voice of each period in which Gregorian chant flourished—either through the continuity of a given tradition or through the influence of different choir masters.

The recordings of my choir in 1960 and 1970 represent the personal response and contribution by myself and Francisco Javier Lara to the continuing evolution of Gregorian chant. Like so many other musicians over previous centuries, we have prepared our own arrangements of these ancient works, so that the Choir of the Benedictine Monks of Santo Domingo de Silos can sing the liturgy according to our own style of performance.

When I took over the Choir of Silos, having completed four years of study at the Abbey of Solesmes, I made significant changes to its choral technique and introduced a series of substantial modifications to the music, particularly in relation to the interpretation of the rhythmic structures. In my opinion, the neumes of

As a child in southern Ohio growing up in the sixties, I would peruse the tiny classical music section of the local library, where I came upon my first album of Gregorian chant. I would listen to it for hours, usually late at night. I continue to listen to these wonderful sounds when I need a break from modern day noise. They assist me in turning inward for meditation and contemplation. Their simplicity helps me turn off this age of anxiety in which we now live. It is a musical form that continues to enrich our lives.

Patricia Wheelhouse

COMPOSER, CHORAL AND
VOCAL MUSIC TEACHER

ancient notation, or square notation, do not allow the singer sufficient musical freedom to touch twentieth-century sensibilities. Therefore, the monks have learned to sing the pieces with measured rhythm.

I directed the Choir of Silos for many years, work that has since been continued by Francisco Javier Lara. Over this period, the enormous interest in the Choir's work has led us to offer the public various recordings. The tessitura, the rhythmic impetus, the blending of tone, the way in which the syllables are divided, the ebb and flow of the music, the phrasing, etc.—all are influenced by our personal understanding of the music.

Without some secure performance guidelines and the fusion of the various elements mentioned above, I believe that the delicate strands of the Gregorian tapestry would have little significance for the twentieth-century audience. ■

A Selection of Chant Recordings

by Peter Jeffery

PLAINCHANT IS THE music of the medieval Christian church, both Eastern and Western. As plainchant developed in the West, local traditions emerged in Spain, Ireland, France, and Italy. Some traces of these early chant traditions remain in manuscripts, although Irish Celtic chant is lost.

Gregorian chant, which replaced local chant traditions in the West, itself evolved into local rites (Sarum chant in England), and was reformed or revised several times. One reform culminated near the end of the nineteenth century with the chant editions of the Benedictine monks of Solesmes, France, who "reformed" chant and returned it to what was perceived to be its original purity. Recent research has thrown into question many aspects of the Solesmes interpretation, and the results have been presented by several performing ensembles.

For an illustration of the Solesmes approach: *Gregorian Chant*, by the Choir of the Monks of Saint-Pierre de Solesmes, Accord 20088a (four CDs). The famous *Chant* CD falls in this category, although the monks of Silos have also recorded some Old Spanish, or Mozarabic chant (Archiv 2533163, LP only). *Chant, Songs of the Spirit*, the new recording by the Gregorian Chant Choir of Ismael Fernandez de la Cuesta, packaged with this book, also contains some Mozarabic chant.

For approaches that revise the Solesmes tradition: *Les Tons de la Musique*, Ensemble Gilles Binchois, Harmonic Records H/CD 8827; *Chants des Voutes Cisterciennes*, Ensemble Venance Fortunat-A.M. Deschamps, L'empreinte digitale ED 13006/Adda AD 184.

A hodgepodge collection (with text-only liner notes), but mid-priced, is *The Tradition of Gregorian Chant* (various monastic ensembles), Archiv 435032-2 (four CDs).

A sampling of Eastern European chant comes from Hungary: *From Evening to Evening*, Schola Hungarica, Hungaroton HCD 31086.

The recording of early chant traditions is the specialty of The Ensemble Organum: *Messe de Saint Marcel* (Old Roman chant), Harmonia Mundi HMC 901382; *Chants de l'Eglise Milanaise*, Harmonia Mundi HMC 901295; *Chants de la Cathedrale de Benevento*, Harmonia Mundi HMC 901476. *Cant de la Sibilla*, by La Capella Reyal-J. Savall, Astree E8705, offers another, very old repertoire. *Missa in Gallicantu*, by the Tallis Scholars (Gimell 017), presents England's Sarum rite chant.

The Eastern half of Christendom developed its own liturgy as well. Byzantine chant is presented in the following CDs: *Passion and Resurrection*, Soeur Marie Keyrouz, Choir of Saint-Julien le Pauvre, Harmonia Mundi HMC 901315; *Liturgy of Saint John Chrysostom*, Greek Byzantine Choir, Lycourgos Angelopoulos, Opus 111 OPS 30-78; *Liturgy of Saint Basilius*, Choir of the Abbey of Chevetogne, Art et Musique CH/CD 105389.

Other traditions: *Christmas, Passion and Resurrection* (Lebanon), Soeur Marie Keyrouz, Choeur et ensemble instr. de la Paix, Harmonia Mundi HMC 901350; *Melchite Sacred Chants* (Syria), Soeur Marie Keyrouz, Harmonia Mundi HMC 901497; *Early Russian Plainchant* (seventeenth century), Patriarchal Choir of Moscow, Opus 111 OPS 30-79; *Ancient Orthodox Chants* (Bulgaria, Greece, Ukraine), Drevnerousski Choir, Chant du Monde LDC 288033. ∎

Contributors

Richard Crocker, Professor Emeritus, University of California at Berkeley, is an internationally recognized musicologist and expert in the fields of Medieval Music and the History of Music. He was Chairman of UC Berkeley's Department of Music from 1975 to 1978. His published books include *A History of Musical Style*, and *The Early Medieval Sequence*, which won the Otto Kinkeldey Prize of the American Musicological Society.

Margot Fassler is a specialist in the chant and liturgy of the Latin Middle Ages. She is currently Director of Yale University's Institute of Sacred Music, and a Professor in both the Yale Divinity School and the Yale School of Music. Her book *Gothic Song* won the Otto Kinkeldey Prize of the American Musicological Society in 1994.

Ismael Fernandez de la Cuesta, former Benedictine monk and Choir Director of the Abbey of Santo Domingo de Silos, Spain, is President of the Spanish Musicology Society and Professor of Musicology at the Royal Conservatory, Madrid. He tours and records with his choir, the Gregorian Chant Choir of Ismael Fernandez de la Cuesta.

Peter Jeffery is a Gregorian chant scholar and Professor of Music at Princeton University. He is a former Oblate of St. Benedict at St. John's Abbey.

Thomas Moore is a leading lecturer and writer in North America and Europe in the areas of archetypal psychology, mythology, and the arts. His best-selling books include *Care of the Soul*, *The Planets Within*, and *Dark Eros*. He is a former Catholic monk who holds a Ph.D. in Religious Studies from Syracuse University and an M.A. in Musicology from the University of Michigan.

Dr. Kenneth R. Pelletier is a leader in the field of holistic health medicine and the author of seven books on the subject, including the best-seller, *Mind as Slayer, Mind as Healer*. He is the Director of the Stanford Corporate Health Program and a Clinical Associate Professor of Medicine at the Stanford University School of Medicine. Since 1979 he has been the President of the American Health Association.

Timothy Rayborn is a musician and scholar working on his doctorate at the University of Leeds, England, where he teaches courses in the Department of Theology and Religious Studies. He is the Director of Florata, a medieval music ensemble whose first CD, *Magnificentia Iberica, Music of Medieval Spain*, was released in September 1995.

CONTRIBUTORS

Don Randel is a Professor of Musicology and renowned scholar of Gregorian chant. Dr. Randel is the Provost of Cornell University.

Huston Smith, author and lecturer on the history of religion, is Professor of Comparative Religion at the University of California, Berkeley. His classic book, *The World Religions*, originally published as *The Religions of Man*, has sold more than one and a half million copies and influenced generations of students.

Bruno Stablein is a musicologist, historian, and authority on the ancient monasteries and convents of Spain.

David Wakely is a San Francisco-based architectural photographer whose work has appeared in numerous architectural design journals. He has also photographed many religious and cultural sites in France, Italy, Greece, Turkey, and the American Southwest. His books include *A Sense of Mission: Historic Churches of the Southwest* and *Markets of Provence*.

Robert Winter is Chairman of the Music Department at UCLA. He is the author of *Music for Our Time* and the developer of the first music-oriented CD-ROM, *Beethoven*.

Photo Notes

Producers' Acknowledgments

❦

by Bruce and Ellen Marcus

TELEVISION PROJECTS OF any type rarely run a predictable course, even less so with the involvement of six television entities, five languages (including Basque), a four-month production schedule, two three-hour Spanish meals a day, and one bat—the flying kind. Yet despite these obstacles, this project has survived and prospered with the same love and devotion that for centuries has kept Gregorian chant alive and flourishing in the minds and hearts of its followers. Many have said that this project has been blessed. We would add that this project has been blessed with wondrously talented and special participants, all of whom are in part responsible for bringing you inspiring sounds and images.

Finding Sr. Ismael Fernandez de la Cuesta was definitely the most important and meaningful part of the project, as Ismael was the cornerstone upon which we built. Long before we met in September 1994, he had been the musical base of many Gregorian chant recordings. As the Choir Director at the Monastery of Santo Domingo de Silos in the 1960's and 1970's, Ismael made the recording which some twenty years later became the best-selling CD *Chant*. As the press worldwide was focusing on the monks at Silos during the summer of 1994, we were looking internationally for new, music-oriented television projects. We immediately thought that Gregorian chant would make an interesting topic for a television documentary and decided to track down the former monk responsible for its current popularity and whom we knew to be in Spain—a country that we visited often and that was the focal point of Ellen's education and language capabilities.

For the previous three summers we had attended a guitar festival in Cordoba, Spain, where our son Evan studied classical guitar with renowned guitarist and longtime friend Pepe Romero. Pepe introduced us to vihuela player and Professor of Musicology John Griffiths, from the University of Melbourne, who put us in touch with Sr. Fernandez. It was proven to us that timing is everything as we quickly learned that this soft-spoken, humble man—now a Professor at Madrid's Royal Conservatory of Music and recognized as one of the world's leading scholars on Gregorian chant—was looking for a more respectful way of exposing the world to Gregorian chant than the Las Vegas stage show that he and the monks of Silos had been recently offered. Actually, Ismael had left the monastery at Silos in the early seventies. He had recently put together a new choir of thirty men from two towns in northern Spain, Vitoria and Aretxabaleta. We traveled to Madrid that September and discovered that our television goals matched Ismael's plans. Our respect for the music and history of Gregorian chant was well received by a man who had dedicated his life to the art form. We became friends as well as business associates.

The project moved at its own pace, dictated both by our ability to attract television partners from the United States and our success at forming relationships in Spain, primarily with Turespana, the Tourist Office of Spain, and Television Espanola (TVE), Spanish television's main network. In November 1994, we held a planning meeting in New York City with Ismael, Professor Don Randel (Dean of Arts and Sciences and now Provost of Cornell University), and Barry Stoner, our co-executive producer and director. Don Randel, a musicologist and expert on Gregorian chant, studied at Silos when he was a graduate student and has been a close friend of Ismael's for decades. As they tell it, in the 1960's, they would retrieve ancient manuscripts from the library at Silos and study all night long by candlelight. We wanted Barry Stoner on the project based on his previous work in Public Television and his inquisitive and calm demeanor, which would play an important role in dealing with the experts and the Spanish. Coincidentally, it turned out that Barry had spent a portion of his advanced education in the seminary—the pieces were falling into place.

In January and March 1995, we returned to Spain to meet with Jaime-Axel Ruiz of Turespana and Federico Llano and Luis de la Barrera of TVE. Jaime-Axel embraced the project as the perfect method to spread knowledge of Spanish culture to the United States. Federico and Luis were intrigued by the vision of their first major co-production with an American company. Without the initial support of these three gentlemen, the project would not have proceeded. Also, on our trip to Madrid in March, we attended an international conference on Gregorian chant and met two other experts from the United States who would later be tapped as part of our program: Professor Margot Fassler, Director of the Yale Institute of Sacred Music, and Professor Thomas Kelly of Harvard.

PRODUCERS' ACKNOWLEDGMENTS

From the beginning, we wanted the project to reach far beyond television. We would record a new CD, produce a video version of the television show, and bring the Choir to the United States on tour. In June we approached Jim Scalem, Public Broadcasting's head of fund-raising programming, to consider airing our one-hour special during the December 1995 pledge drive. We huddled at Public Broadcasting's annual meeting with Jim and with David Othmer, Station Manager at WHYY-TV in Philadelphia, the Public Television station that would become co-producer and partner. Jim and David brought Public Television into the project with considerable financial and moral support. It didn't hurt that David has grown up in South America and speaks fluent Spanish.

This book itself is the outgrowth of interest in the project, from the onset, by Mark Powelson and Pamela Byers of KQED Books & Video, San Francisco. KQED saw the potential and joined Public Television and WHYY.

With the funding and broadcast outlet in place, we went to Spain once again to finalize planning with TVE and Turespana. David, Barry, and Suzanne Duroux (our Associate Producer) accompanied us as we spent one week visiting potential locations and hashing out a production schedule with TVE and the Choir. We were assigned a TVE field producer, Miguel Sainz, who—after we departed for the States—spent countless days driving all over northern Spain searching for the perfect monastery for our videotaping.

Ironically, to remember the audio recording of such beautiful music, one must first recall a collection of irritating sounds. The Monastery of Santa Maria la Real in Aguilar de Campoo has arguably the best acoustics of any of the 300 or so monasteries and Romanesque churches in northern Spain. The Center for Romanesque Studies, based in Aguilar de Campoo, oversees the restoration of all these churches and monasteries in addition to running a quaint inn that managed to book a biker convention on the weekend we planned to record the Choir. Someone also forgot to tell us about the well traveled road not more than twenty feet from the main chapel. (Juan Carlos Prieto Vielba, the inn's Director, was truly a gracious host, housing and feeding the Choir and crew at an incredible discount.) Our previously calm and now frazzled recording engineer, Michael Seberich, joined Barry Faldner, our music producer from Chicago, in deciding that our new recording schedule would be from midnight until 6:00 a.m. The Choir—fundamentally creatures of the night—were thrilled, as were the bats, who generally count on the late evening hours to catch up on their flying exercises.

Over the next three weeks Miguel Sainz, his wife Ana (a producer at TVE), and Miguel Martin, the director of the soon-to-open Cervantes Institute Office in Chicago, labored to obtain permission for us to tape in a number of locations in Spain. The plan for the last week in September was to have Barry Stoner, Suzanne Duroux, and Larry Neukum (our Director of Photography from Los Angeles) travel from Madrid northward with Miguel and a small crew from TVE. They would capture on tape the exteriors and interiors of many monasteries and churches, including the Monastery of San Juan de Los Reyes, the Cathedral of Toledo, the Cistercian Monastery of Santa Maria de Huerta in Soria, and the Royal Convent of Las Huelgas in Burgos. We were also joined by David Wakely, a photographer from San Francisco retained by KQED to document the project with still shots. Ultimately, they would meet us at the primary location for our videotaping, the Basilica and Pantheon at the Monastery of San Isidoro in Leon. The authentic twelfth- and thirteenth-century venues of San Isidoro proved to be the ideal location for the Choir.

The end to the chronicle of our journey should not diminish the efforts that were made upon our return by Barry and WHYY-TV to get the program edited and onto Public Television in December in more than 150 cities across the United States. A special addition to the program was the inclusion of several minutes of an interview with Cardinal Bevilacqua of Philadelphia, who graciously agreed to be interviewed. The entire technical team performed superbly amid the continual barrage of schedule changes, interruptions, and unanticipated problems. Ismael and the Choir held up so well that they are now set to tour the United States in 1996. Their newly recorded CD and video will be distributed worldwide along with the television program itself. As for the two of us, we are making plans with Ismael and his wife Choni to exchange our teenage sons for the summer—a much more manageable venture.

ELLEN MARCUS
BRUCE MARCUS

The Gregorian Chant Choir of Ismael Fernandez de la Cuesta

M	Ismael Fernandez de la Cuesta (Director)
A	Angel Barandiaran (Assistant Director)
V	Antxón Lete (Assistant Director)
V	Beñat Abajo
A	Iñaki Agirre
A	Imanol Aizpurua
A	Iñigo Aizpurua
A	Txomin Arana
A	Aitor Aranzábal
V	Alberto Basterra
A	Jokin Bengoa
A	José Cruz Urcelai
V	Formerio Diaz de Otazu
V	Angel Maria Echeverría
A	Miguel Elorza
A	José Luis Errasti
V	Jesús María Estarrona
A	Ricardo Garro
V	Gurutz Larrañaga
V	Julen Larrañaga
V	Alberto Madinabeitia
A	Javier Marcos
A	Carmelo Olabe
A	Iñaki Ortiz de Zárate
V	Ramón Pérez
V	Alberto Rojo
V	Aitor Sáenz de Argondoña
V	Rafael Sevilla
V	Rafael Unzalu
A	Alejandro Urcelai
A	Pedro Urcelai
A	Alberto Uribetxebarria

(M—from Madrid)
(A—from the town of Aretxabaleta, Basque province of Guipuzcoa)
(V—from the town of Vitoria, Basque province of Alava)

Guest soprano Mariatxen Urkia, from Aretxabaleta, sings
Catholicorum concio.

Glossary/Index

High Mass Also known as the Solemn Mass. It requires a choir for the singing of the common and proper of the mass. The gospel is sung and the altar incensed. A modified form of the High Mass, called the Low Mass, is the most common way in which the Mass is celebrated. 86

Hiley, David, 104

Hinduism, 60–63

Hispanic chant A Latin liturgical chant formerly in use throughout the Iberian peninsula but now preserved only in one chapel of the Cathedral of Toledo. Also known as Mozarabic chant, Visigothic chant, and chant of the Rite of Toledo. See *Mozarabic chant*.

I

Iadgari, 41

Ignatius of Antioch, 120

Ildefonse, 17

Introit (Latin, "entrance") The first part of the Mass, consisting of an antiphon, a psalm verse, the *Gloria Patri*, and the antiphon repeated. 14, 38, 45, 152

Isidore, Bishop of Seville (560-636) A scholar of heroic capacity, Isidore's collecting of Greek and Roman writings helped assure their survival and transmission to the West. In 622, he published the *"Originum sive etymologiarum libri XX,"* an encyclopedia of the arts and sciences. 17, 45

Islam, 74–77

J

Jeffery, Peter, 10, 35–55, 132

Josquin des Pres (c.1440-1521) A composer and singer from the north of France, considered the greatest composer of the high Renaissance, the most varied in invention and the most profound in expression. He was a master singer in ecclesiastical choirs in France, Milan, and Rome. 25

Judaism, 23, 67–68

K

Kelly, Thomas, 8

Kitaro, 89

Kyrie Eleison (Greek, "Lord have mercy") 1) An invocation sung by the choir at High Mass after the introit. 2) A musical setting of the same. *Kyrie eleison*, repeated thrice, occurs frequently in the Roman liturgy, usually in association with the Lord's Prayer. 46, 51

Kyrie fons bonitatis, 152

L

La Messe de Nostre Dame, 50

Lara, Francisco Javier, 129

Las Huelgas, 123

Lassus, Orlande (c.1530-1594) Franco-Flemish composer. One of the most prolific and versatile composers of the sixteenth century, Lassus wrote over 2,000 works, including masses, motets, songs, hymns, and psalms. He combined expressive Italian melody, elegant French text-setting, and northern polyphony with his own imaginative responses to the texts. 25

Latin Latin is the former language of Latium, the Italian provinces around Rome. During the third century, it superseded Greek as the language of the Western Church. Latin remains the official language of the Catholic Church although, especially since the Second Vatican Council, local vernacular has become dominant in liturgical and extra-liturgical worship and in the training of the clergy. 12, 23, 55, 69, 112

Lauds (Latin, "praises") The dawn prayers of the Divine Office, usually said with Matins, consisting of four psalms and a canticle, with their antiphons, followed by variable hymns and verses, then the *Benedictus*, with its antiphon, then commemorations and conclusion. 45, 108

P

Palestrina, Giovanni Pierluigi da (c. 1525-1594) Italian composer, organist, music teacher, and master singer. A prolific composer of masses, motets and other sacred music, as well as madrigals, Palestrina ranks as one of the greatest Renaissance composers. He is known for a seamless polyphony in which all voices are perfectly balanced. So great was his reputation in his own time that in 1577 he was asked to rewrite the Catholic Church's main plainchant books, following the Council of Trent's guidelines. His most famous mass is the *Missa Papae Marcelli.* 25, 26, 54

Patrologia Latina, 18

Patronage system, 50

Pelletier, Dr. Kenneth R., 10, 85–97

Peper, Erik, 2

Plainchant Vocal music sung at the same pitch; rhythmic, not metrical—an extension of speech rather than of verse. In its ecclesiastical form as Gregorian chant, it is the official music of the Catholic Church's liturgy. The modes (or scales) of the chant are confined to the natural intervals of the human voice and the melodies to its natural range. There is no chromatic scale or chromatic progression and, normally, no modulation from one mode to another in the same melody. Individual notes are generally equal in time length but the speed of singing may be fast or slow according to the will of the singers. Characteristic of plainchant are the use of two choirs singing the same melody alternately and the use of a reciting note upon which short melodies frequently repeated are dependent. Its beauty depends largely upon voice quality and rhythmical subtlety. 56

Plausas A Latin word indicating praise and approval. 128

Plotinus, 8

Polyphony A term derived from the Greek for "many voiced," used for music in which two or more strands sound simultaneously. The term "polyphonic era" is generally applied to the late Middle Ages and the Renaissance; the kind of polyphony used in the Baroque era, by Bach and Handel, is usually described by the term "counterpoint." 13, 25, 47, 50, 54, 56, 69, 128

Pope Gregory I, 74, 97

Pope John XXII, 50

Pope Pius X (1835-1914) Pope from 1903 to 1914. In his 1903 encyclical *Motu Proprio*, he called for the use of Gregorian chant throughout Catholic services. Declared a saint in 1954. 55

Pothier, Father, 22

Power, Leonel (c.1375-1445) A choir master and leading English composer of the fifteenth century. With his younger English contemporary, John Dunstaple, he was a pioneer of the unified mass cycle, having taken the initiative in pairing movements of the Ordinary. The Ordinary cycle *Alma redemptoris mater* is ascribed to him. 51

Prado, German, 18

Proper of the Mass Those parts of the Mass that are variable according to the day or feast being observed; the introit, gradual, alleluia, gospel, offertory, and other parts. When the Mass is sung, each of these parts are sung.

Prose see *Sequence.* 45

Psalm 1) One of the biblical hymns collected in the Book of Psalms. 2) A version of one of the psalms used as a liturgical hymn. 12, 23, 25, 29, 35, 108

Psalmody 1) The act of singing psalms in worship. 2) The arrangement of psalms for singing. 38, 108

Ptolemy, 79

Public Broadcasting Service, 149

Pueri cantores, 122

Pythagoras, 79

The Songs of the Spirit come alive in a classic tour of northern Spain

TAKE AN INSIGHTFUL TRIP with public broadcasting to northern Spain to experience the cultural, historical, and musical world of Gregorian chant. Unique excursions await you in the Spanish country side–from Moorish castles and walled cities to extraordinary musical presentations in ancient monasteries, as seen in the public broadcasting special, "Gregorian Chant: Songs of the Spirit".

TOUR HIGHLIGHTS INCLUDE:

- Exquisite accommodations at many of Spain's four and five star Paradors throughout the region
- The medieval city of León including the Basilica and Pantheon at the Monastery of San Isidoro and the 13th century cathedral, a masterpiece of Gothic architecture
- The famous monastery of Santo Domingo de Silos where chants are still regularly sung by the community of monks
- The walled city of Segovia featuring the Roman Aqueduct dating back to the 1st century
- Quality regional cuisine throughout northern Spain including private group tours of local wineries
- Post-tour option: A weekend in Madrid, including a half-day tour of the Prado Museum, and deluxe stay at the Hotel Palace

Feel the cobblestone beneath your feet and the sounds of chant in your ears in this customized tour of northern Spain created exclusively for members of public broadcasting.

Photos: Corel®

FOR COMPLETE TOUR DETAILS, CALL 1-800-685-9446

Participation in this tour will benefit many local public broadcast stations throughout the United States.

Compact Disc Program Notes by Ismael Fernandez de la Cuesta

THE CHANTS IN this performance of the Mass are sung with discant. *Discantos* are ornamentations that were placed above the fixed melody of a plainchant.

The codices that contain the pieces we are including in this Mass are from a period in history during which musicians imposed many theories that would permit a measured rhythmic interpretation of chant. This measured, rhythmic form of chanting helped create the necessary consonance by superimposing an invented melody upon a plainchant. But the technique of discant existed before music theorists decided—based upon a standard application of fixed rhythmic modes—to assign a rhythmic superstructure to these chants from the thirteenth and fourteenth centuries. That is why we have tried to go far back in time to discover the free musical rhythm with which Gregorian chant was undoubtedly sung before a precise rhythm was imposed upon the plainchant and its *discanto*.

We are thus reintroducing a way of singing Gregorian chant that until now had been lost.

This program represents a reconstruction of the musical portions of a Mass of Saint Mary. The chants derive from various repertories of the twelfth through fourteenth centuries.

During the Middle Ages, special holy day masses were entirely chanted. By saying "chanted" I also mean to say "recited." Many centuries ago, chanting was understood to include recitations of prayers, readings of Biblical passages, and acclamations. The Mass we are presenting here does not contain these recitatives—only the chants of the Proper of the Mass (*Introit, Gradual, Alleluia, Offertory*) and of the Ordinary of the Mass (*Kyrie, Gloria, Sanctus, Agnus Dei*). During the Renaissance, and into modern times, these chants from the Ordinary became part of the polyphonic mass.

CD SELECTIONS

Mass of the Blessed Virgin Mary (Missa de Beata Maria Virgine)

1.   *Salve Sanctia Parens* Introit (Mode II)
2.   *Kyrie fons bonitatis* Litany with trope and discant (Mode III)
3.   *Gloria spiritus et alme* Hymn with trope and triple discant
4.   *Benedicta et venerabilis* Gradual responsory with discant (Mode I)
5.   *Alleluia. Salve Virgo* Alleluia with discant (Mode VIII)
6.   *Recordare. Ab hoc Familia* Offertory with discant and trope (Mode IV)
7.   *Sanctus. Te laudant* Acclamation with trope and discant (Mode VIII)
8.   *Agnus Dei. O Iesu Salvator* Litany with trope and triple discant (Mode V)
9.   *Beata viscera* Communion (Mode I)

Marian Antiphons

10.   *Ave regina caclorum* Marian antiphon (Mode VI, transposed)
11.   *Regina caeli* Marian antiphon (Mode VI)
12.   *Salve Regina* Marian antiphon (Mode I)
13.   *Alma redemptoris mater* Marian antiphon with double bourdon (Mode V)

Some Feasts of the Virgin had their specific chants for the Mass. But for the celebration of other holy days—and particularly for the commemoration of Mary, which was observed on all non-festival Saturdays (except during the Easter period)—the Choir Master would choose chants from a common Marian repertory, depending on the liturgical times and the local custom. Although certain chants of the Ordinary of the Mass such as *Kyrie fons bonitatis* did not have to be sung on the Feast of the Virgin, nothing in its music or Trinitarian theme would prohibit its being chosen. ■